Peterborough Ontario
Book 3 in Colour Photos,
Saving Our History
One Photo at a Time

Photography
by Barbara Raué
2015

Series Name:
Cruising Ontario

Book 101: Peterborough Book 3

Cover photo: Peterborough Armoury

Series Name: Cruising Ontario
Saving Our History One Photo at a Time
in colour photos

Other Books by Barbara Raue

Coins of Gold

Arrows, Indians and Love

The Life and Times of Barbara
Volume 1: Inventions That Have Enhanced My Life
Volume 2: Entertainment That I Have Enjoyed
Volume 3: East Coast Trips
Volume 4: Olympics Have Always Intrigued Me
Volume 5: Wonders of the World
Volume 6: Caribbean Cruises We Have Enjoyed
Volume 7: Animals
Volume 8: Storms and Other Major Disasters in My Lifetime
Volume 9: Wars, Terrorist Attacks and Major Disasters

The Cromwell Family Book

Laura Secord Discovered

Daddy Where Are You?

Visit Barbara's website to view all of her books
http://barbararaue.ca

Peterborough

Peterborough is a city on the Otonabee River in central Ontario, 125 kilometres (78 miles) northeast of Toronto. Peterborough's nickname of "The Electric City" underscores the historical and present day importance of technology and manufacturing as an economic base of the city which has operations from large multi-national companies such as Seimans, Rolls Royce, and General Electric. Peterborough is known as the gateway to the Kawarthas, "cottage country", a large recreational region of the province. In 1818, Adam Scott settled on the west shore of the Otonabee River and the following year he began construction of a sawmill and gristmill, establishing the area as Scott's Plains. The mill was located at the foot of present-day King Street and was powered by water from Jackson Creek.

The year 1825 marked the arrival of 1,878 Irish immigrants from the city of Cork, a British Parliament experimental emigration plan to transport poor Irish families to Upper Canada. The scheme was managed by Peter Robinson, a politician in York (present-day Toronto). Scott's Plains was renamed Peterborough in his honour. The Irish emigrated from the Emerald Isle to escape over-crowding, poverty, political unrest, religious tensions, disease and the potato famine. By 1851 almost half of the town of Peterborough claimed Irish ancestry. They cleared the land in the rolling hills of the Peterborough countryside

In 1845, Sandford Fleming, inventor of Standard Time and designer of Canada's first postage stamp, moved to the city to live with Dr. John Hutchison and his family, staying until 1847. Dr. John Hutchison was one of Peterborough's first resident doctors.

Beginning in the late 1850s, a canoe building industry grew up in and around Peterborough. The Peterborough Canoe Company was founded in 1893, with the factory being built on the site of the original Adam Scott mill. From 1928–36 the Johnson Motor Company/Outboard Marine (the makers of motorized boat engines) was established as an outgrowth of the original industry.

Peterborough was one of the first places in the country to begin generating hydro electrical power (even before the plants at Niagara Falls). Companies like Edison General Electric Company (later Canadian General Electric) and America Cereal Company (later to become Quaker Oats, and in 2001 PepsiCo, Inc.), opened to take advantage of cheap hydro-electric power.

Bridgenorth

Bridgenorth is located on Chemong Lake in the Kawarthas. It is located north of Peterborough on Chemong Road.

Emerald Isle

Emerald Isle is located on Buckhorn Lake.

Ennismore

Ennismore is located in Selwyn Township in central-eastern Ontario.

Table of Contents

Our Marine Heritage

The Peterborough area is generally regarded as the birthplace of the modern day canoe. Inspired by the First Nations rugged wooden dugouts, and delicate birch bark canoes, several local inventors developed a light but sturdy craft made of basswood or cedar planks during the 1850s.

This and other adaptations launched a world-renowned canoe building industry along the banks of the Otonabee which lasted more than a century. Ironically, technological changed forced industry leaders like the Peterborough Canoe Company to close in the early 1960s. Fortunately Outboard Marine Corporation's former plant remains a tribute to our marine heritage, now serving as the home of the Canadian Canoe Museum.

The Canoe Voyage of Johnny Smith

On June 18, 1934, Johnny Smith set out from the George Street wharf near this point in the *Pride of Peterborough*, a red, specially fitted five metre Peterborough canoe. The goal of this intrepid 24-year-old adventurer from Smith Township, a former merchant seaman and Peterborough Canoe Co. employee, was to be the first person to paddle across the Atlantic in a canoe – to Peterborough, England. After an unprecedented shooting of all the St. Lawrence rapids, he left Gaspe, Quebec July 20 on the 400 kilometre crossing of the Gulf of St. Lawrence to the island of Newfoundland. He never completed the voyage. His body and red canoe were washed ashore on the west coast of that island, and he is buried there.

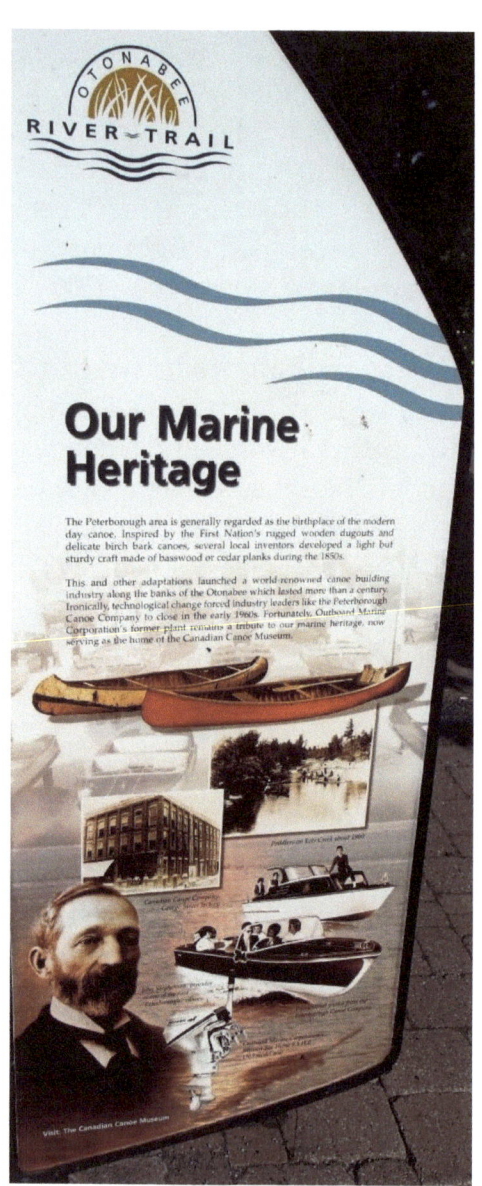

Our Marine Heritage

The Peterborough area is generally regarded as the birthplace of the modern day canoe. Inspired by the First Nation's rugged wooden dugouts and delicate birch bark canoes, several local inventors developed a light but sturdy craft made of basswood or cedar planks during the 1850s.

This and other adaptations launched a world-renowned canoe building industry along the banks of the Otonabee which lasted more than a century. Ironically, technological change forced industry leaders like the Peterborough Canoe Company to close in the early 1960s. Fortunately, Outboard Marine Corporation's former plant remains a tribute to our marine heritage, now serving as the home of the Canadian Canoe Museum.

Visit The Canadian Canoe Museum

Irish Heritage

Following 1825 thousands of relatives and friends of the Robinson settlers and other Irish exiles left their beloved Emerald Isle for the rolling hills of the Peterborough countryside. They emigrated to escape over-crowding, poverty, political unrest, religious tensions, disease, and the potato famine. By 1851 almost half the town of Peterborough's population claimed Irish ancestry.

They cleared the land and these Irish families provided the basis for future generations to move into skilled trades, business and commerce, various professions, politics, and government service. Today we celebrate their Celtic heritage through story-telling, festive gatherings, fiddle music, dancing reels and step dances, and folk songs.

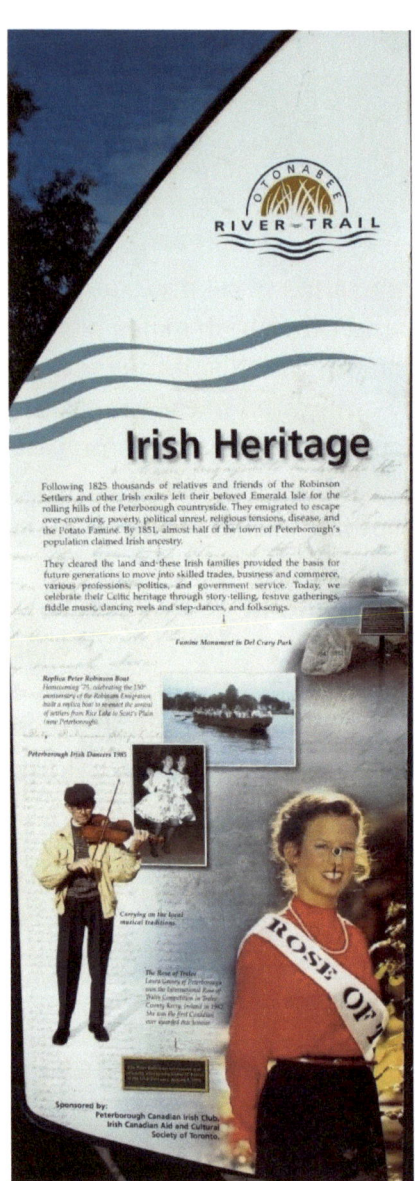

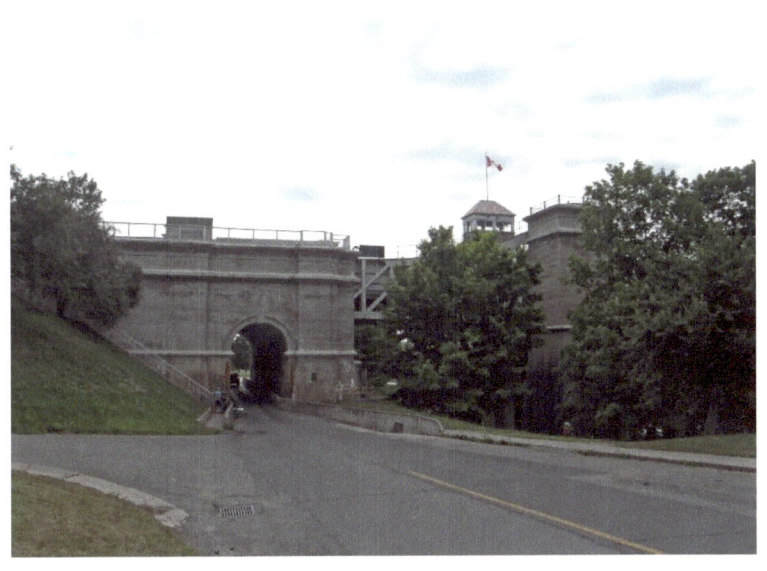

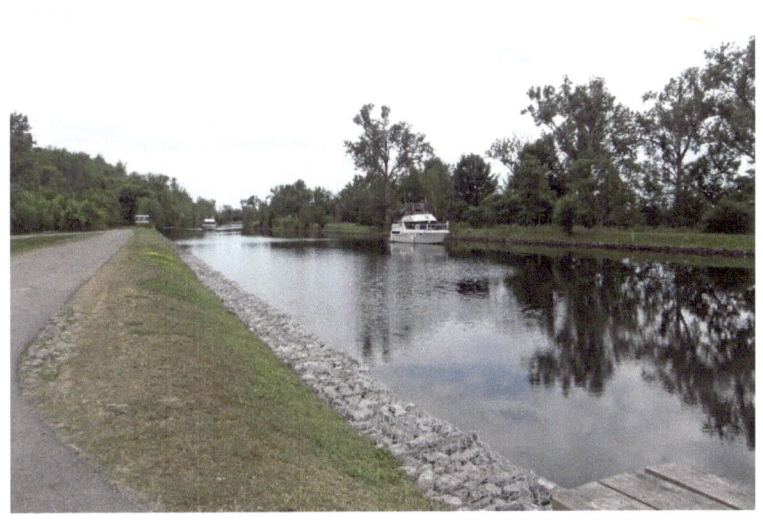

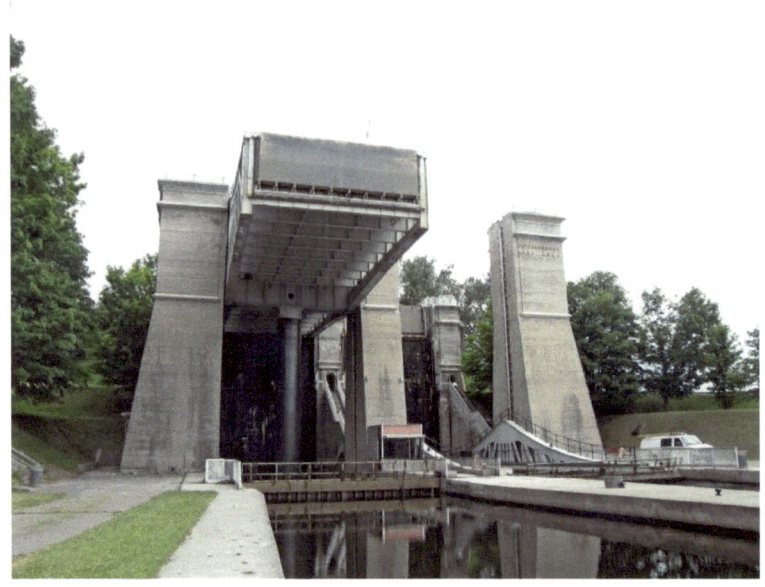

The Peterborough Lift Lock was completed on July 9, 1904. It was the first lock to be built out of concrete and at the time was the largest structure built in the world with unreinforced concrete. It is a boat lift located on the Trent Canal in the city of Peterborough and is Lock 21 on the Trent-Severn Waterway. The dual lifts are the highest hydraulic boat lifts in the world, with a lift of 19.8 m (65 ft).

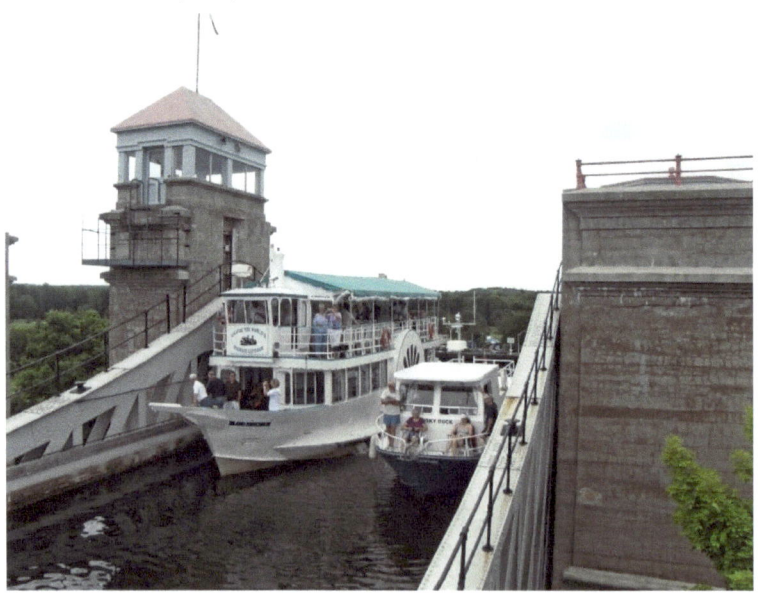

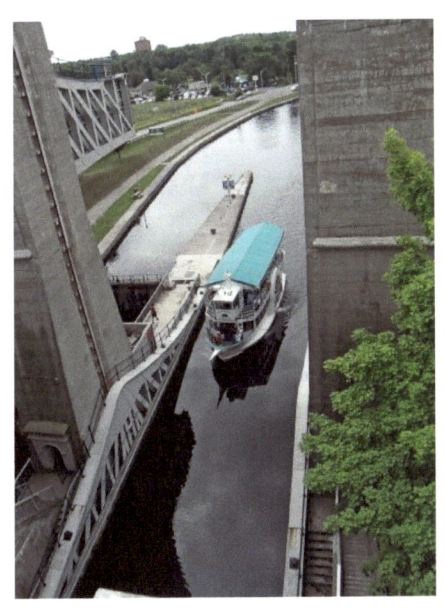

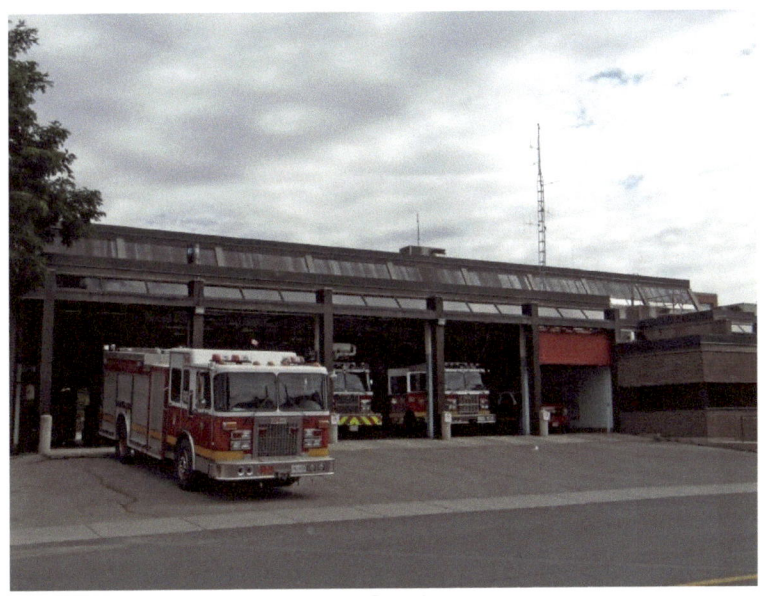

Fire Station

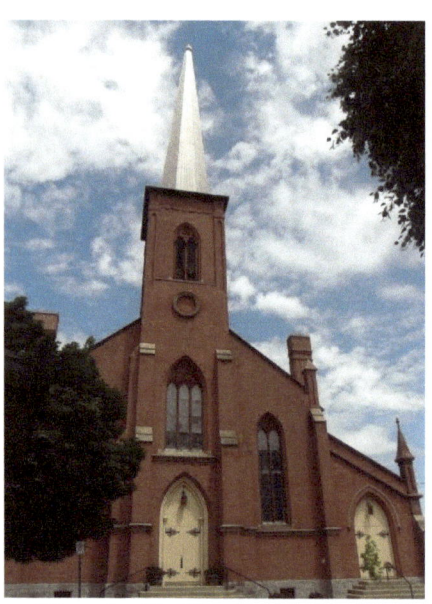

120 Murray Street - St. Paul's Presbyterian Church

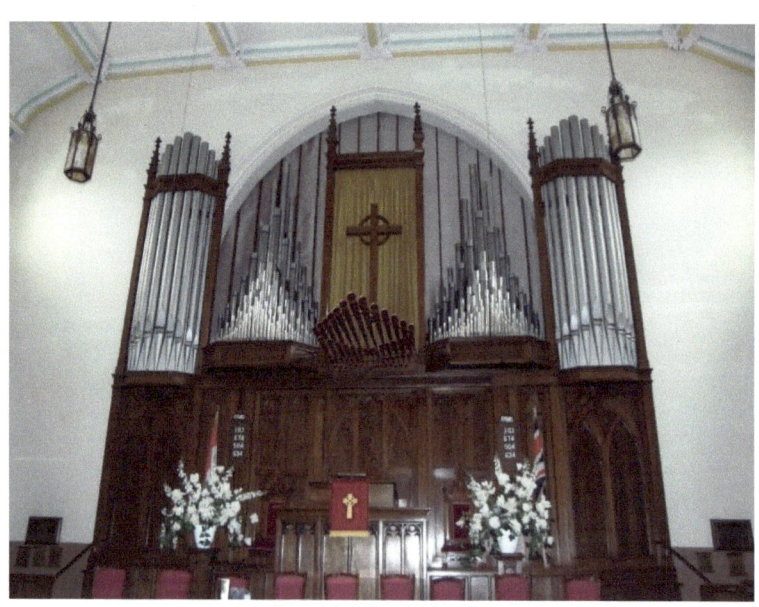

Inside St. Paul's

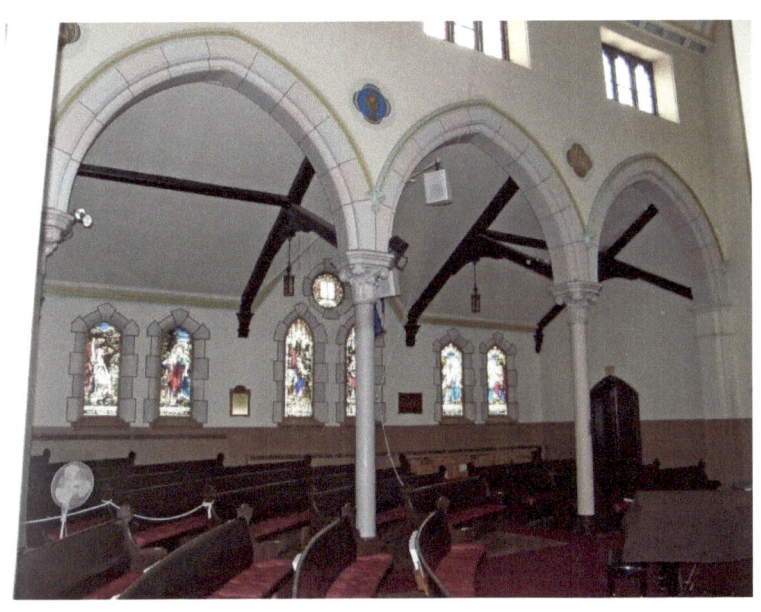

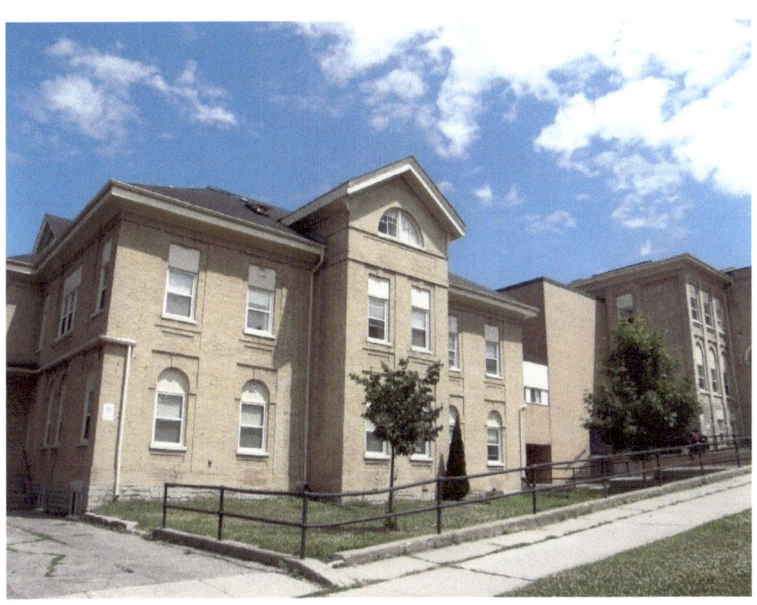

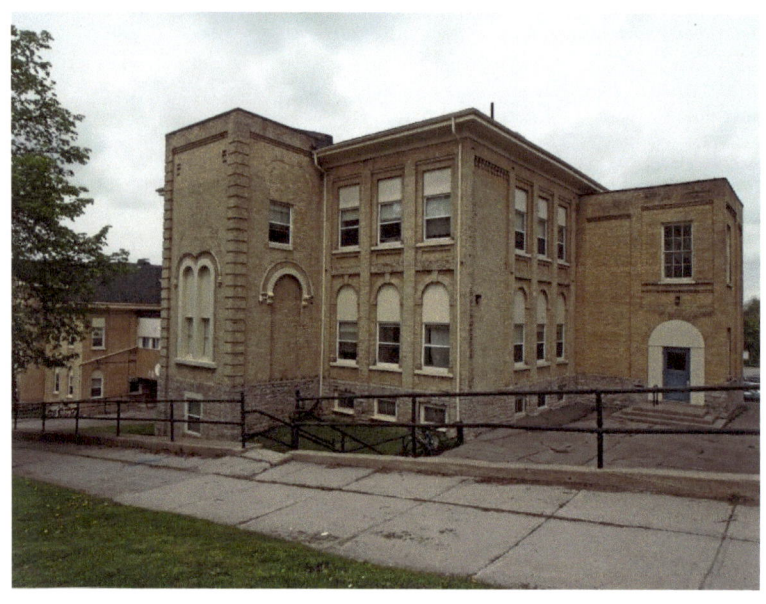

90 Murray Street - Victoria Park Apartments
Romanesque style

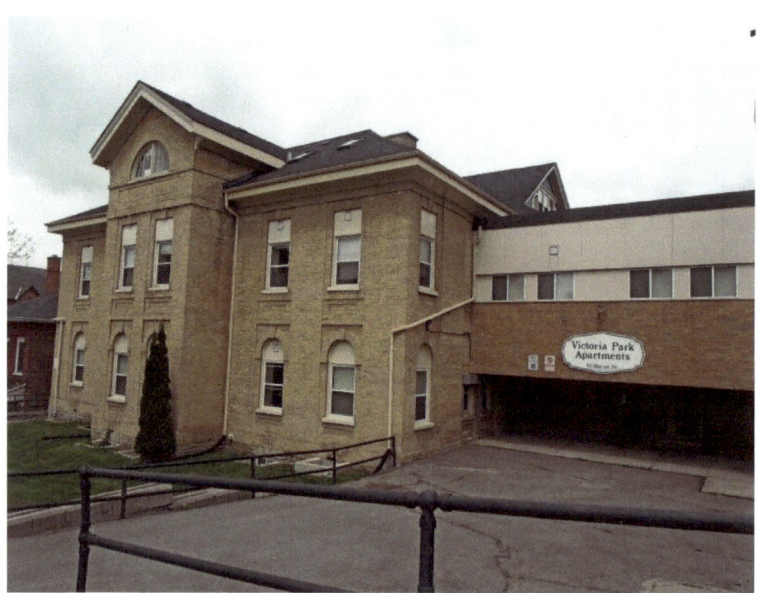

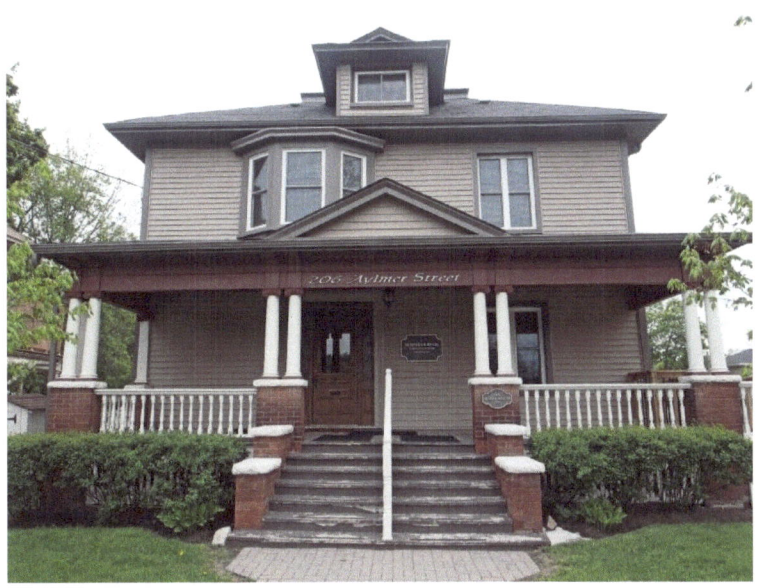

The Madge House – 1837
206 Aylmer Street

Robert P. Madge was a retired English lieutenant of the Royal Navy who originally settled on Sandy Lake in Harvey Township in about 1832. The Madge House is one of the oldest houses in the City of Peterborough. Huge hand hewn timbers were used in the construction of the house, a very large frame house of the 1830s. The Madge House appeared on the assessment rolls in 1838 as a two-storey frame house with one additional fireplace. Robert P. Madge was listed as both the owner and occupant.

The Madge House was originally covered with rough cast plaster. The side windows were French doors opening onto upper and lower verandas which encircled the house on three sides.

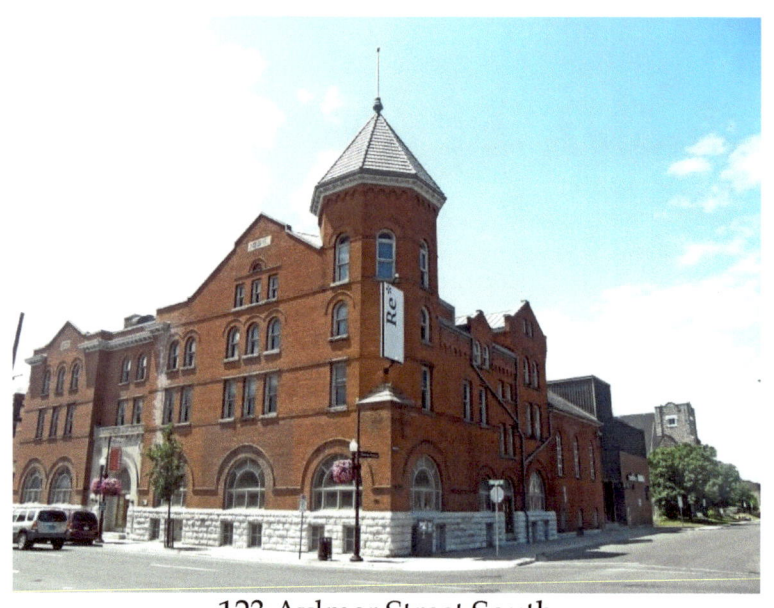

123 Aylmer Street South
Young Men's Christian Association – 1896

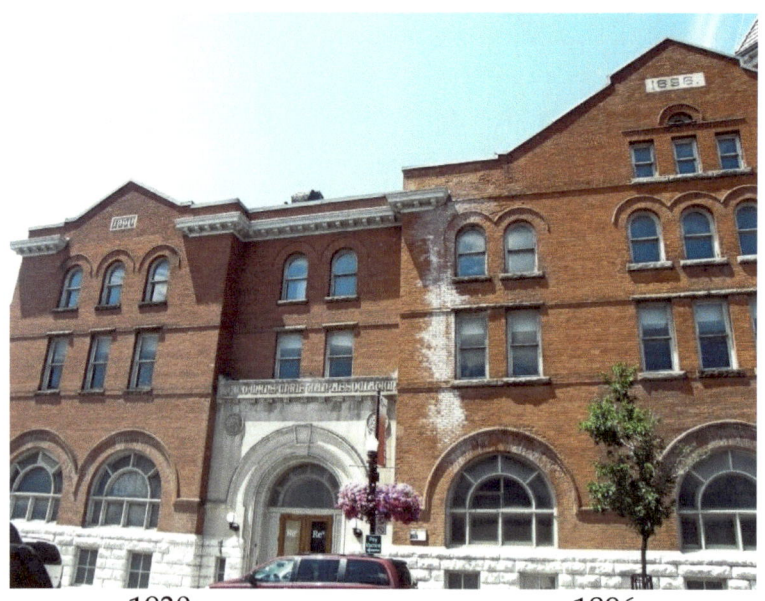

1930   1896

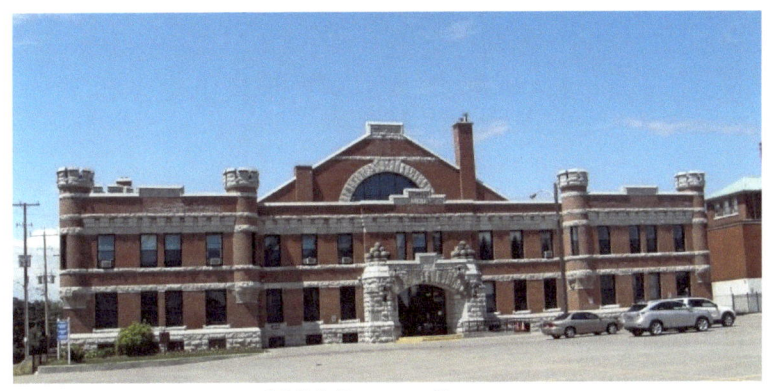

220 Murray Street
Hastings and Prince Edward Regiment Peterborough Garrison

Central Park was an ideal site for a military training area with its expansive grounds and location – accessible by foot, horse and wagon. A drill shed was built in 1867 and used for bank practices, dances and military activities. Drill sheds were built in many communities across Canada after the Fenian Raids of 1866. The shed was destroyed by fire in 1909, just before the Peterborough Armoury was opened on May 24. The Armoury was built during a nation-wide spending program for the militia in response to the Boer War. The Armoury included a parade hall, living quarters for infantry, cavalry, and artillery, a firing range, and a bowling alley.

The Peterborough Armouries were built in the Romanesque style with turrets, arched troop doors, and crenellated roof line.

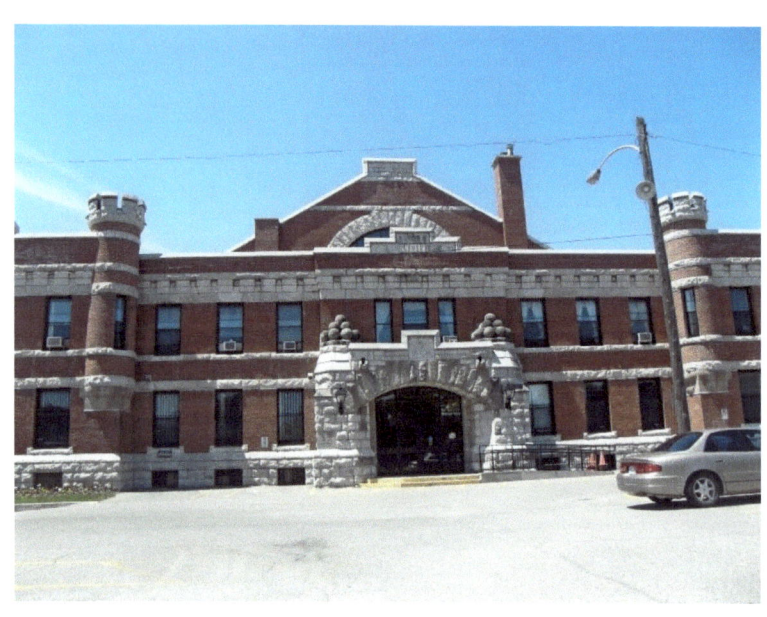

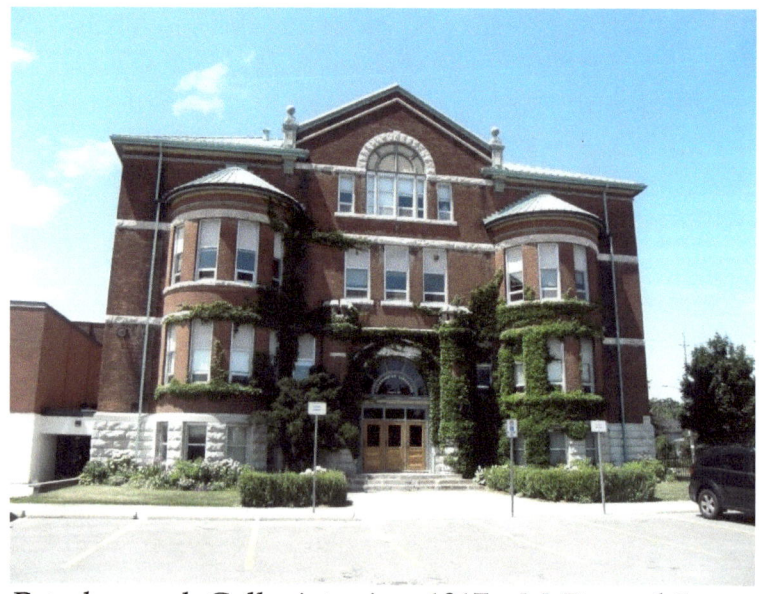

Peterborough Collegiate circa 1917 – McDonnel Street
Romanesque Revival architecture

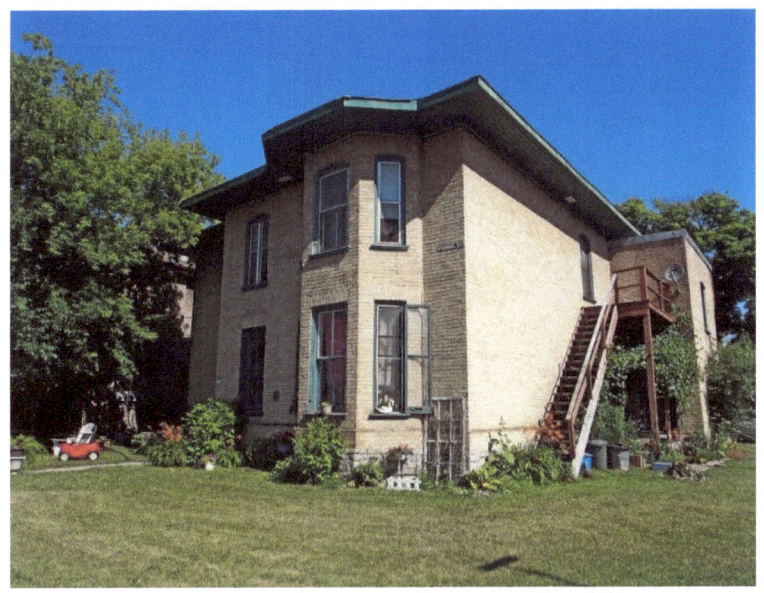

106 McDonnel Street – heritage building

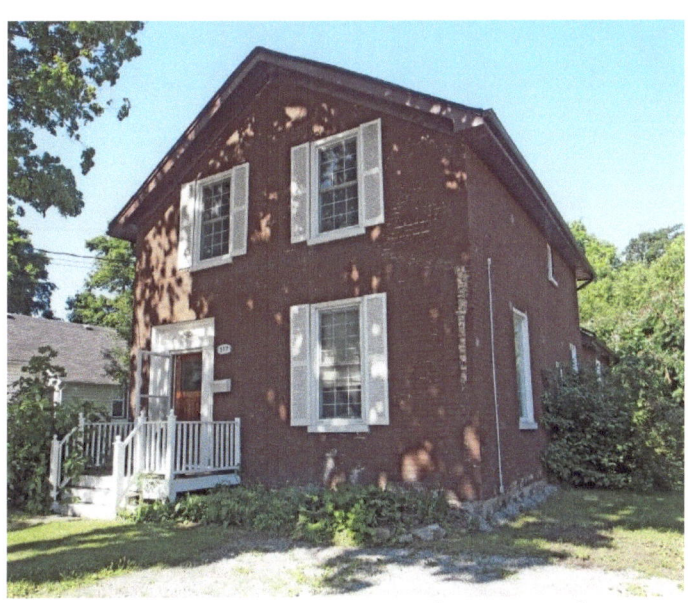

577 Harvey Street – Gothic Revival

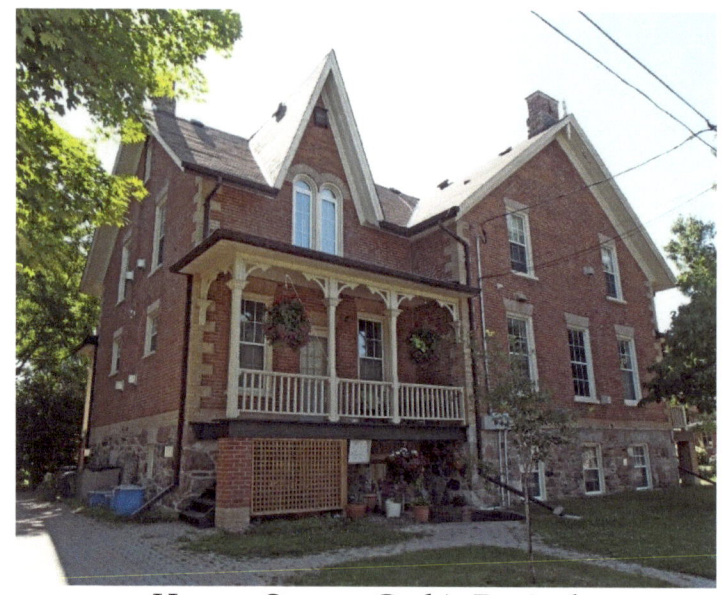

Harvey Street – Gothic Revival

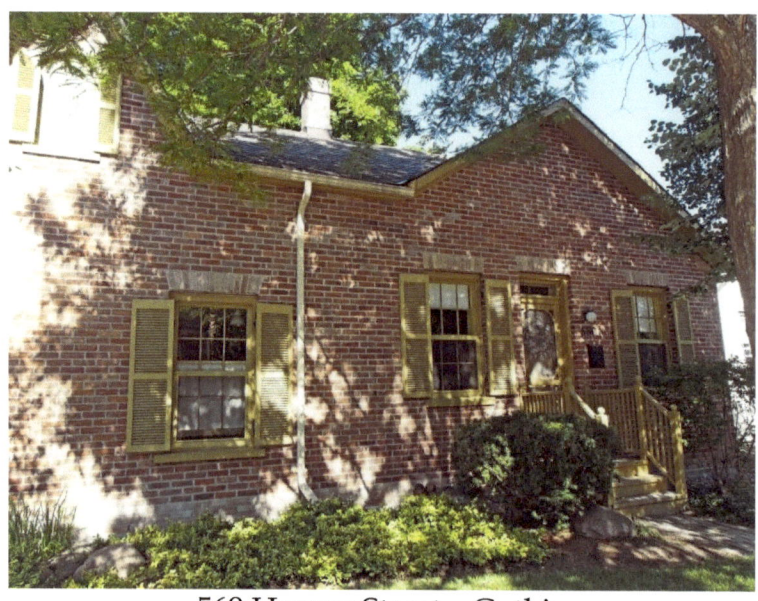

569 Harvey Street – Gothic

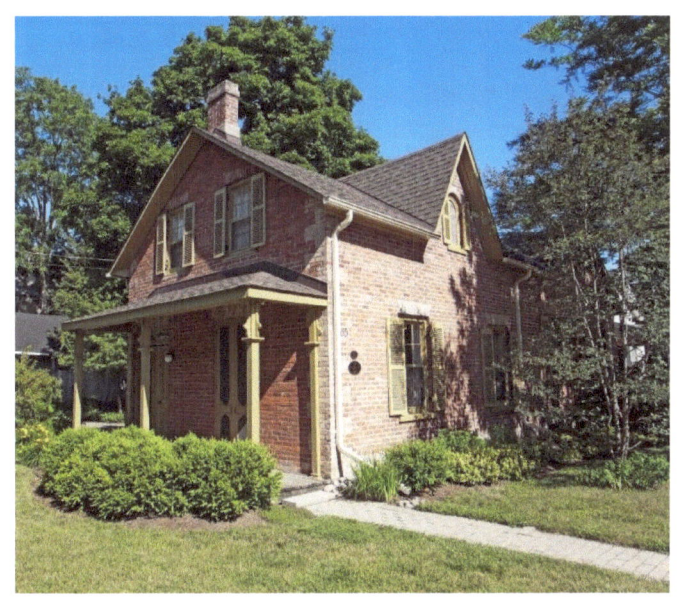

565 Harvey Street

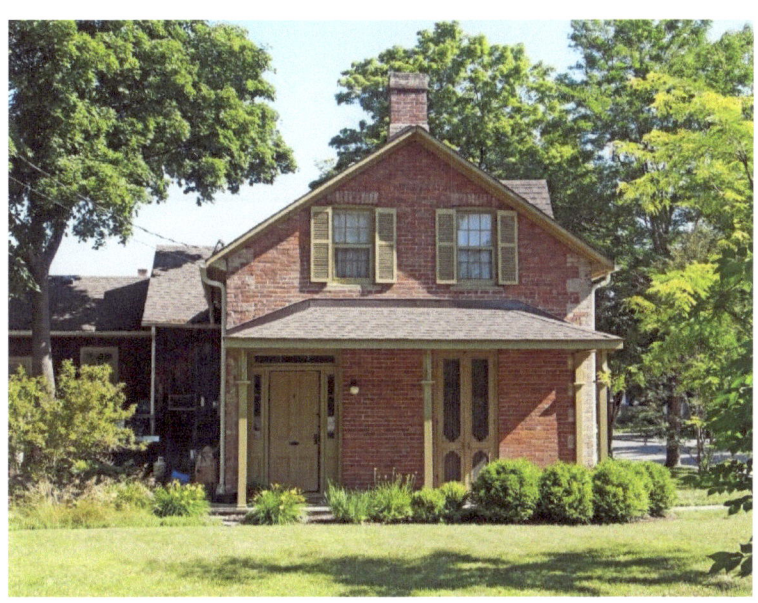

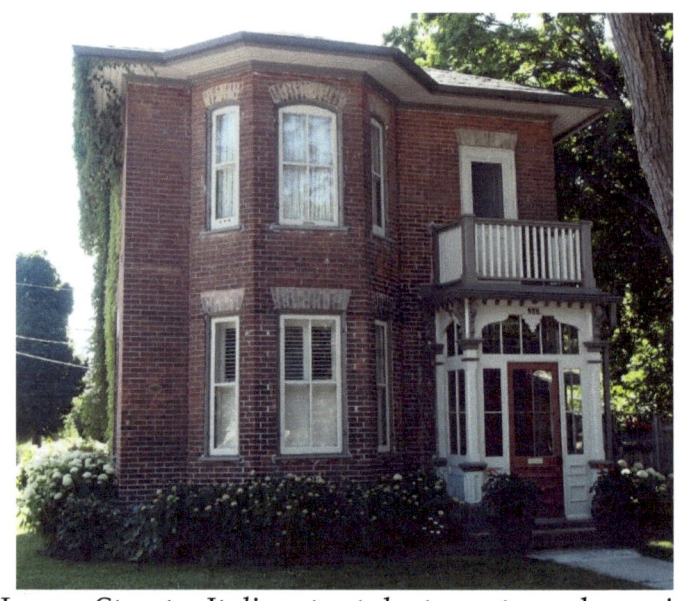

558 Harvey Street – Italianate style, two-storey bay window, balcony on second floor

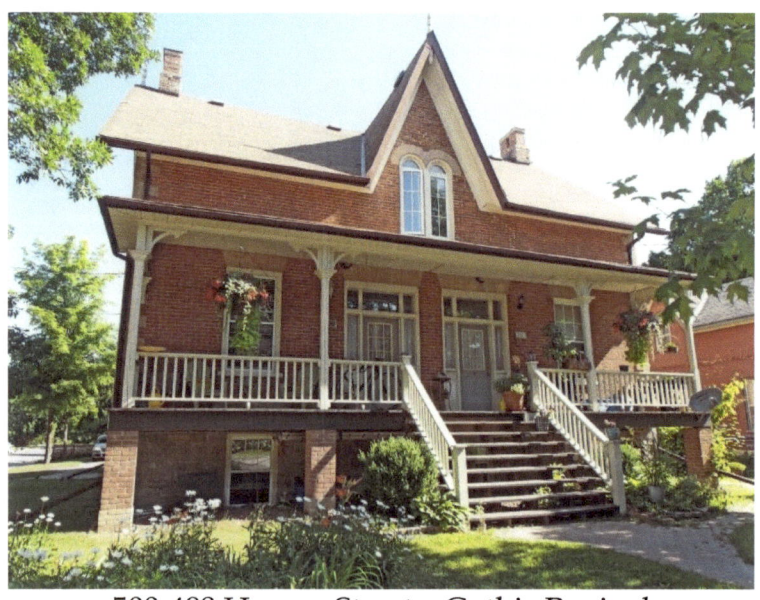

500-498 Harvey Street – Gothic Revival

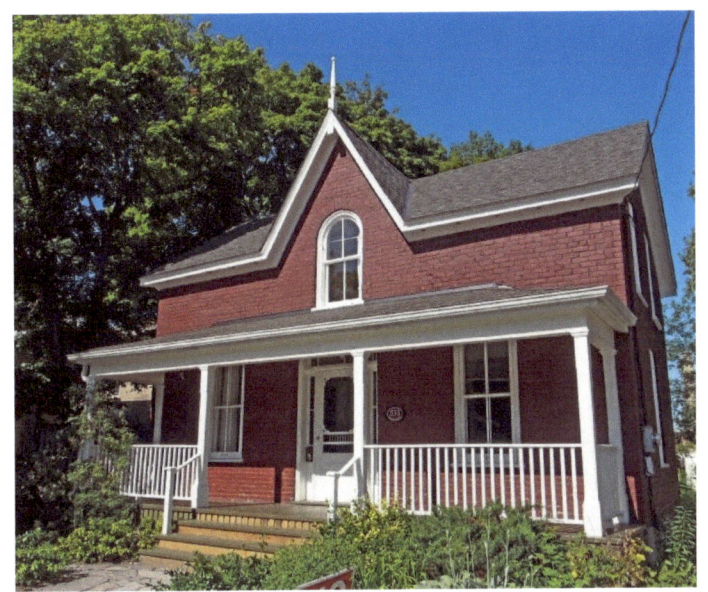

533 Harvey Street – John Britton House c. 1830 – Gothic, finial on gable

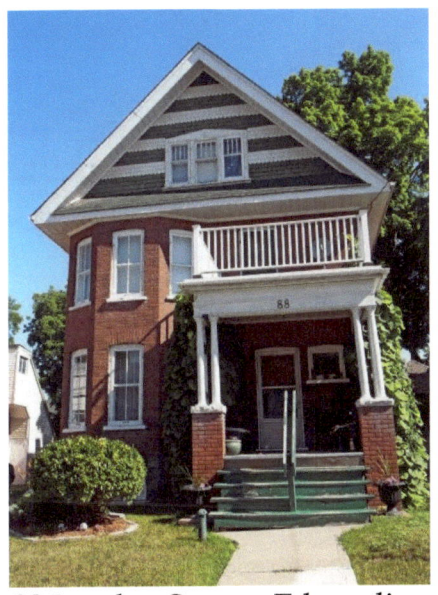

88 London Street - Edwardian

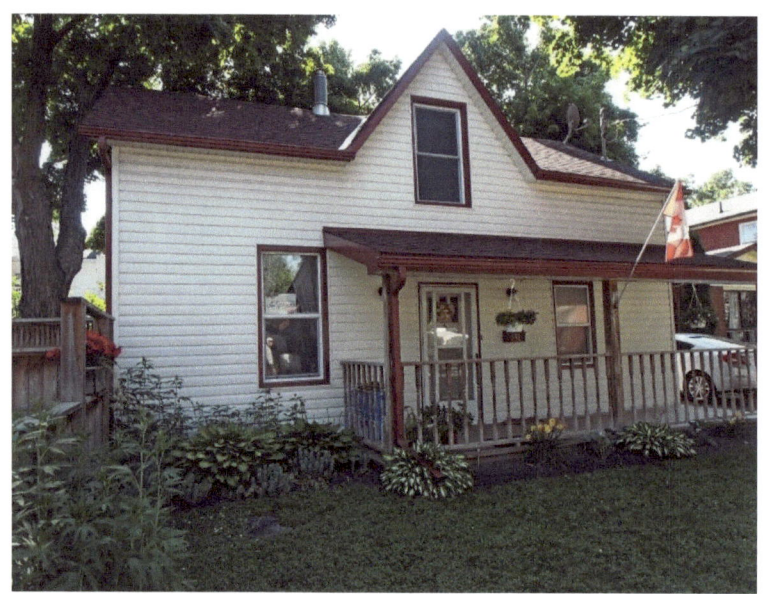

552 London Street – Regency Cottage

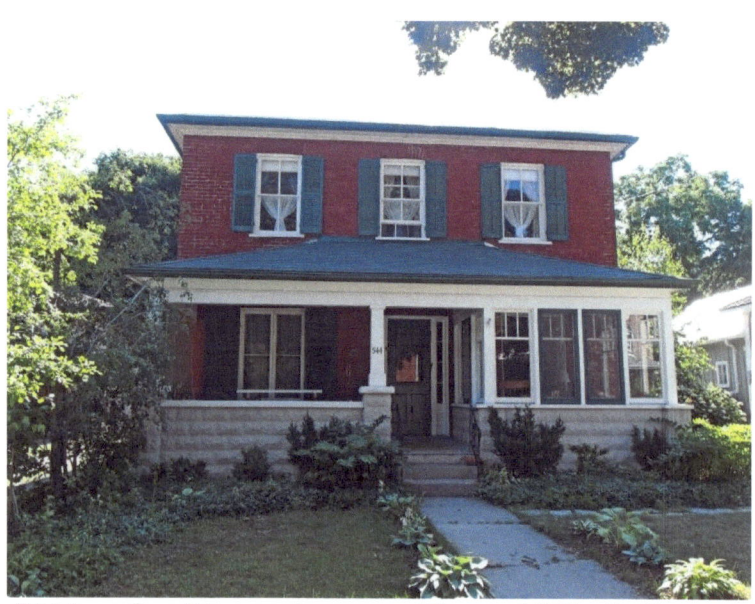

544 London Street – Jameson House 1879 – Italianate, hipped roof

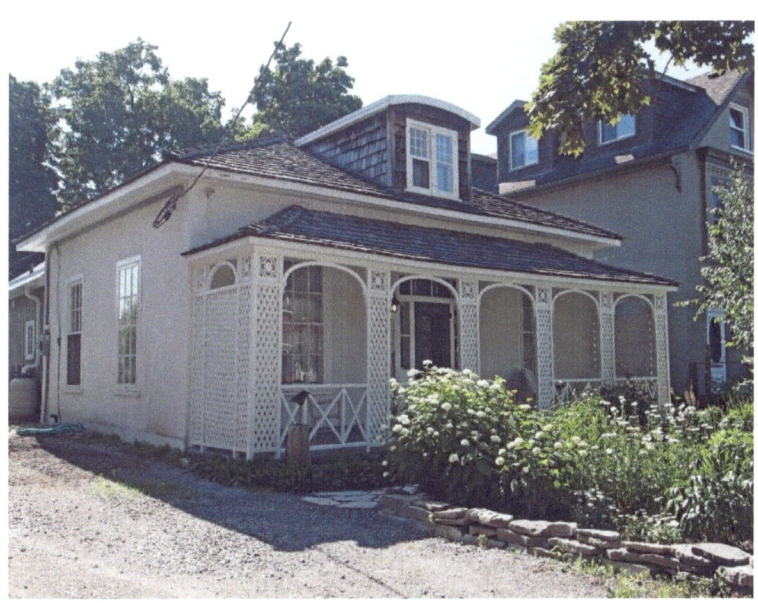

538 London Street – The Henry Myers Cottage 1858, Dormer

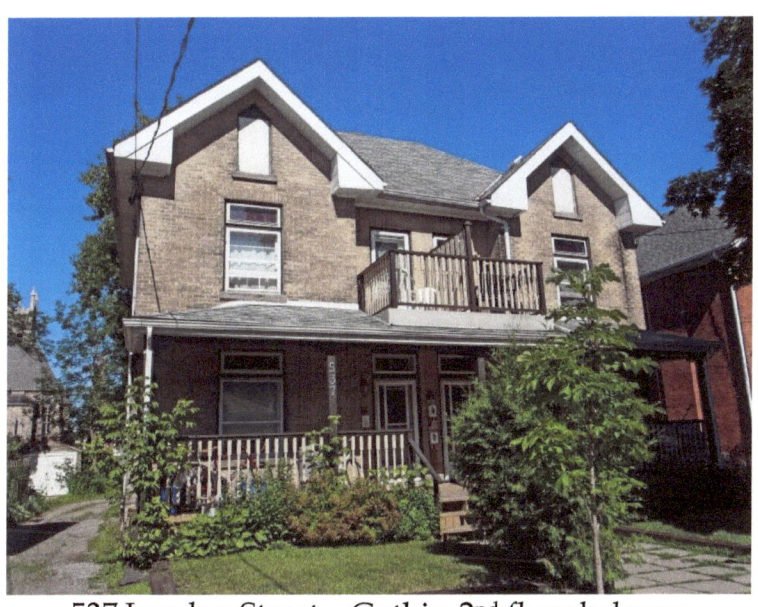

537 London Street – Gothic, 2nd floor balcony

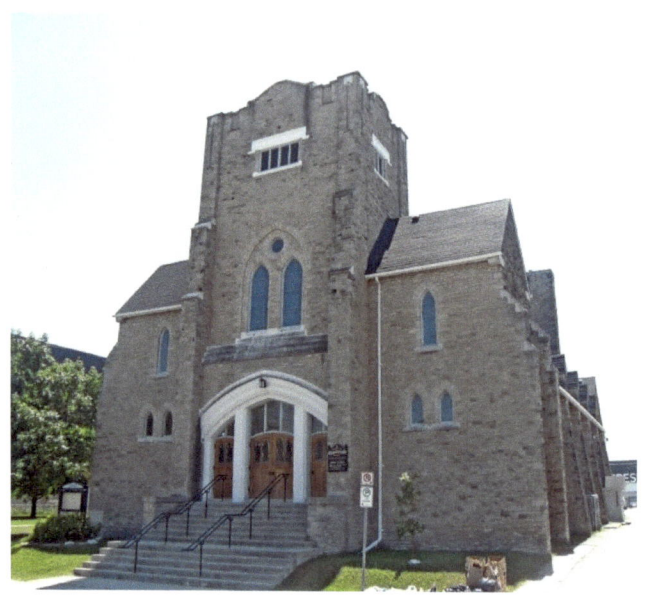

175 Murray Street - Baptist Church – buttresses, lancet windows

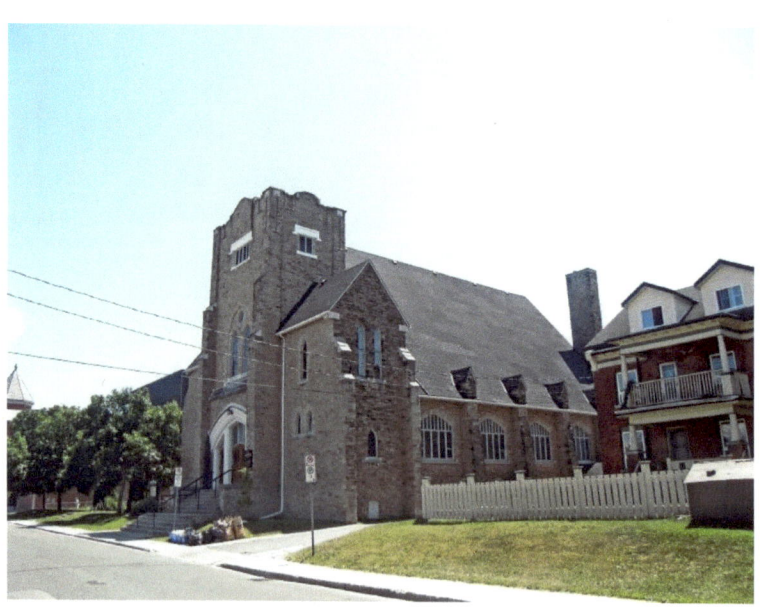

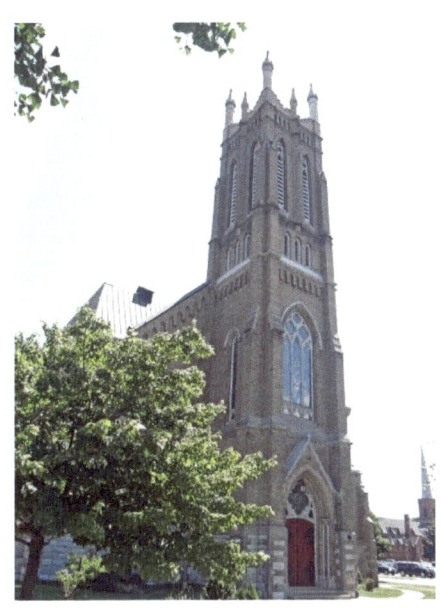

1875 Wesleyan Methodist Church

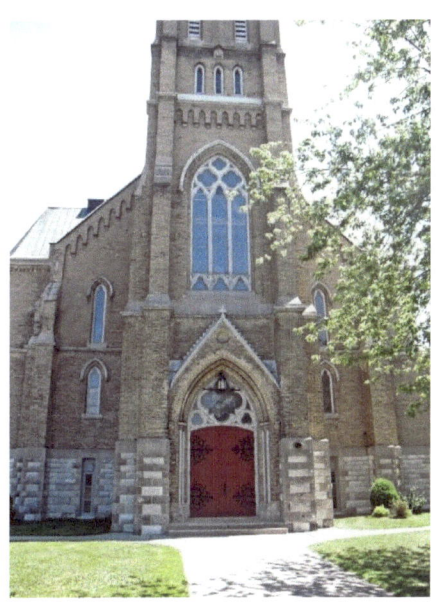

Architrave, rose window

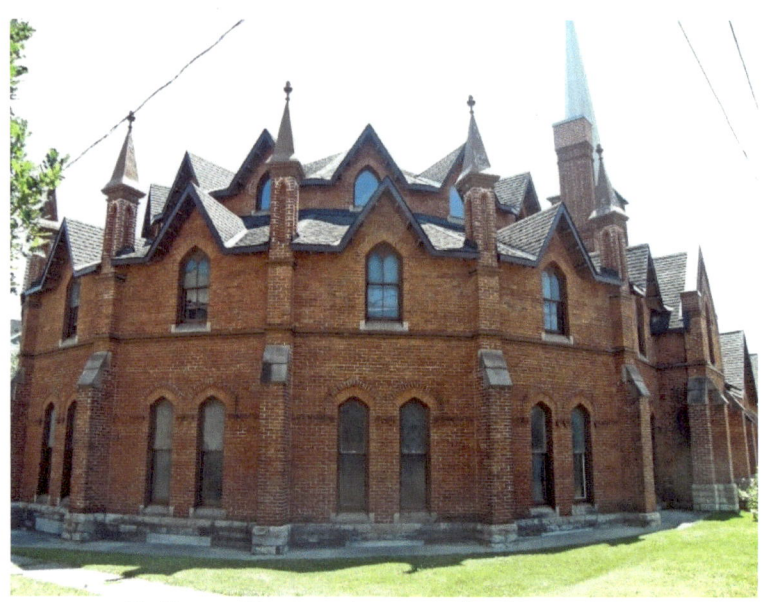

Police – Queen Anne style, buttresses

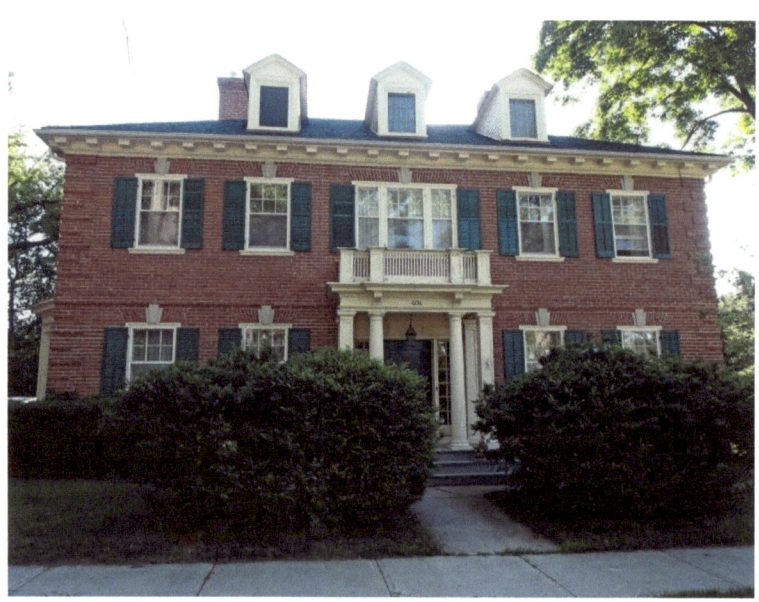

404 Belmont Avenue – Georgian, dormers in attic

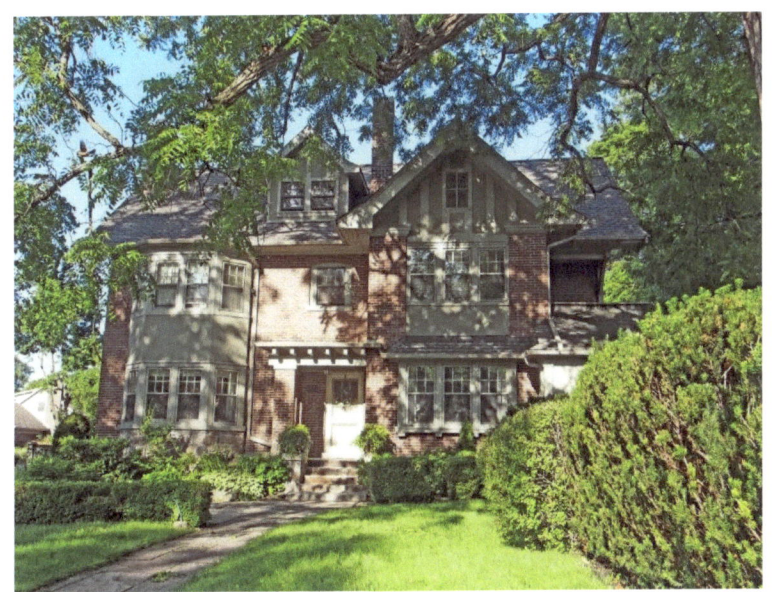

488 Belmont Avenue - Tudor

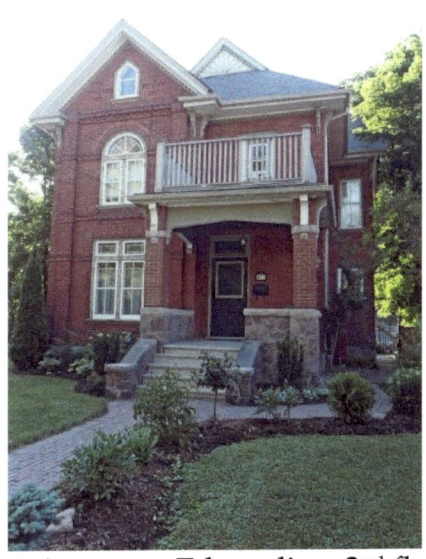

477 Belmont Avenue – Edwardian, 2nd floor balcony

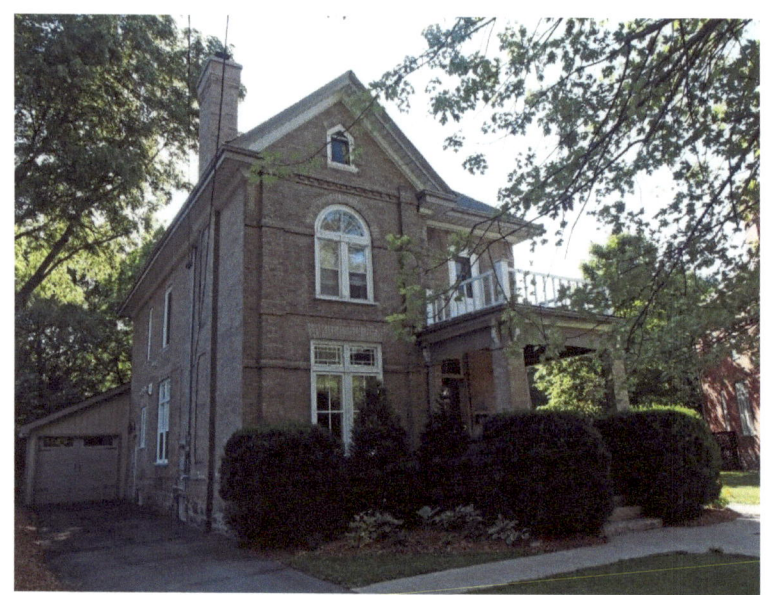

380 Belmont Avenue – Gothic Revival, banding, 2nd floor balcony

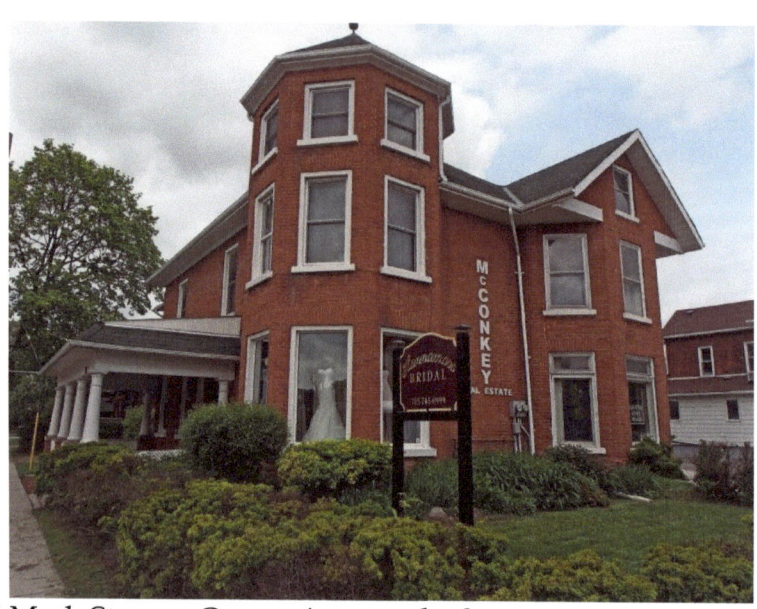

406 Mark Street – Queen Anne style, 3-storey tower, 2½ storey tower-like bay with cornice return on gable

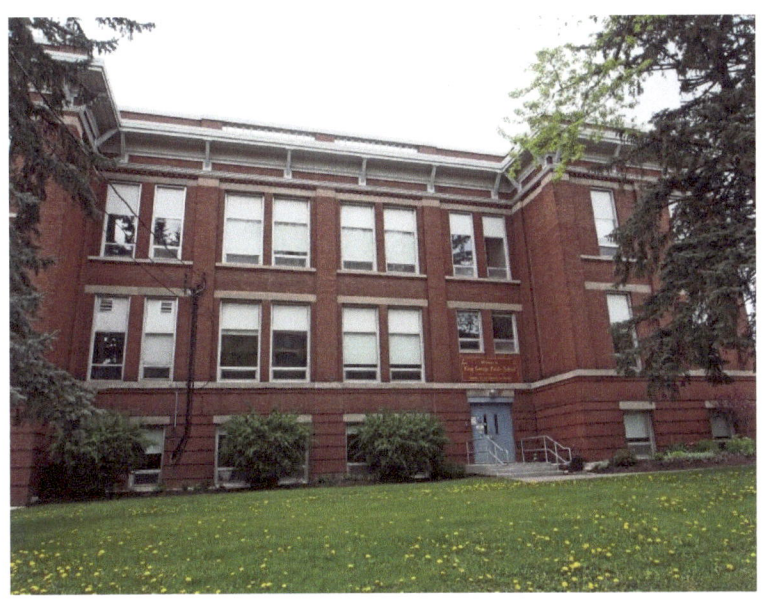

Hunter Street East - King George Public School

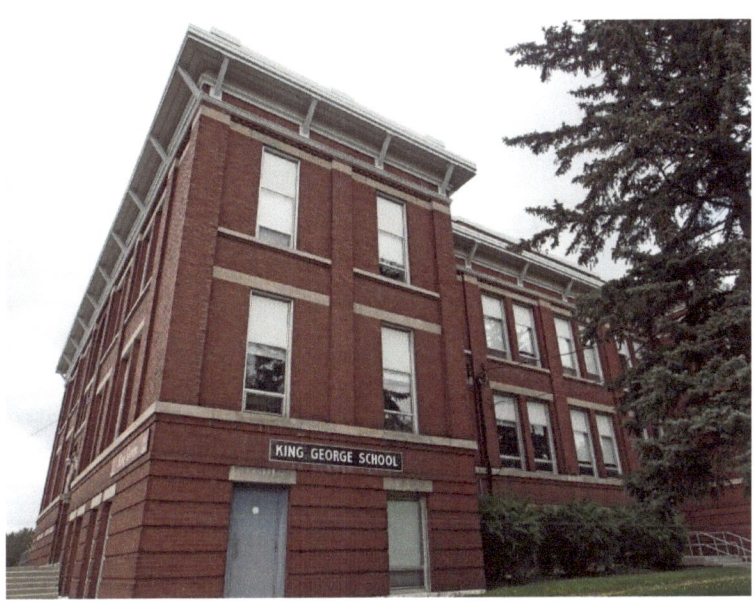

King George Public School

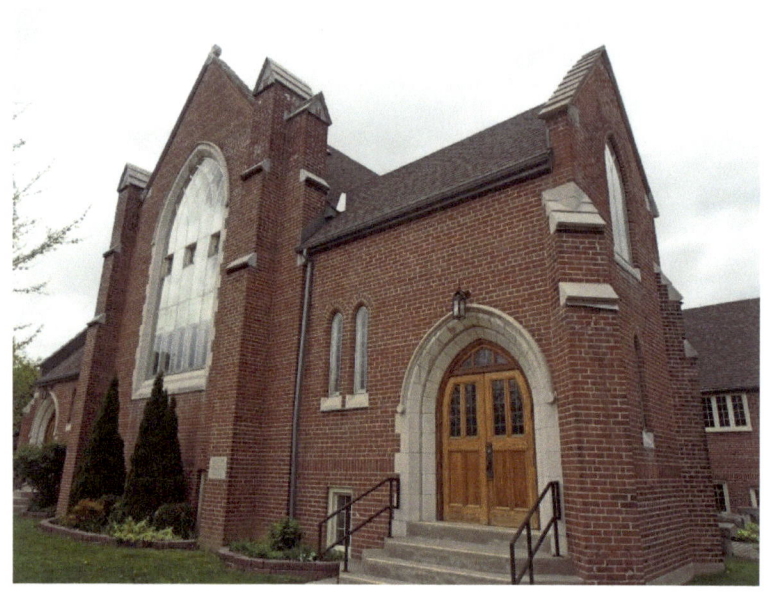

90 Hunter Street East (corner of Mark Street)
Mark Street United Church – A. D. 1928

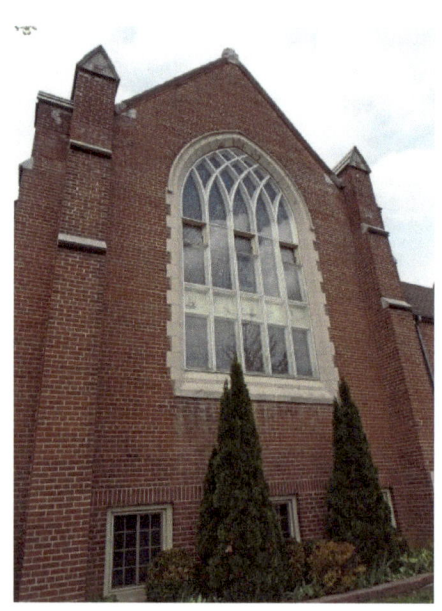

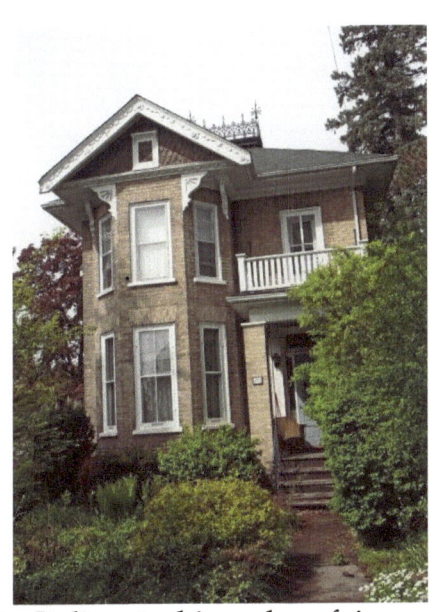

351 Park Street – Italianate, hipped roof, iron cresting on roof, fretwork, 2nd floor balcony, 2½ storey tower-like bay

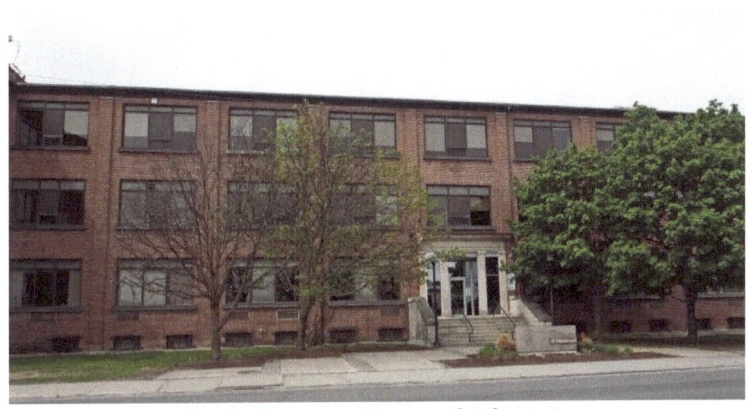

Park Street - General Electric

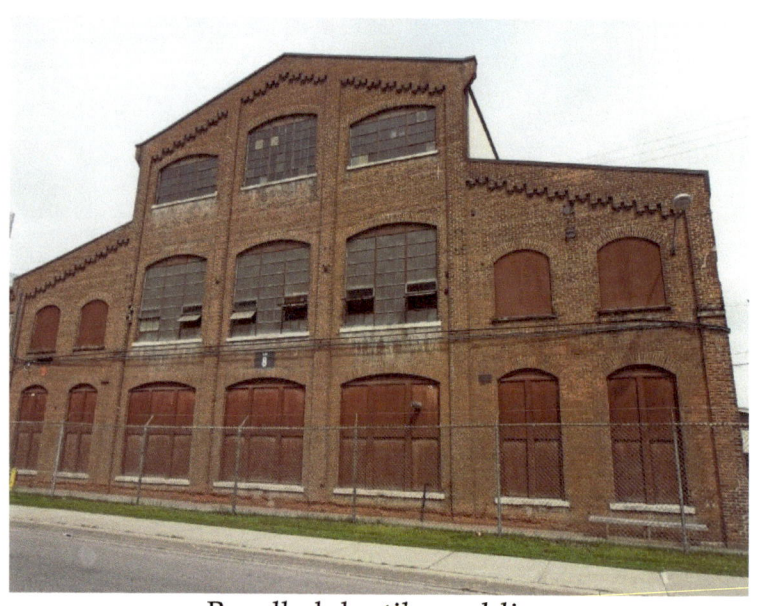

Bevelled dentil moulding

General Electric

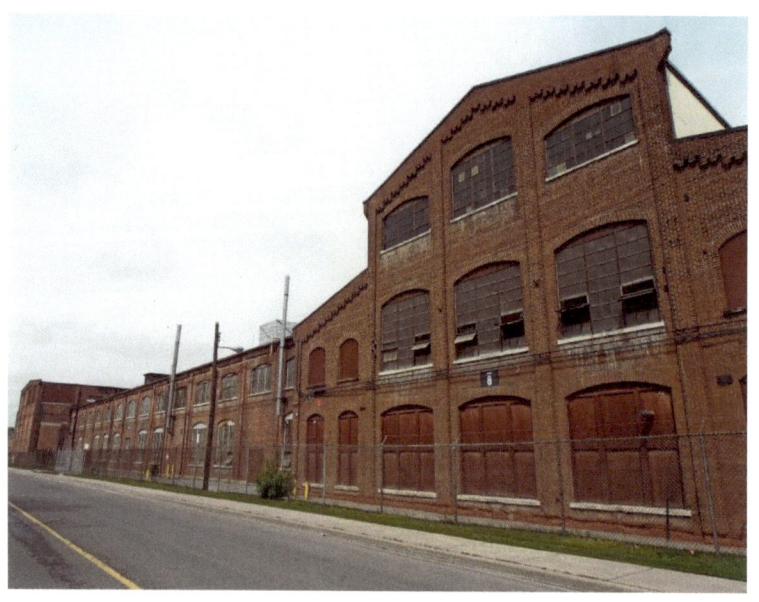

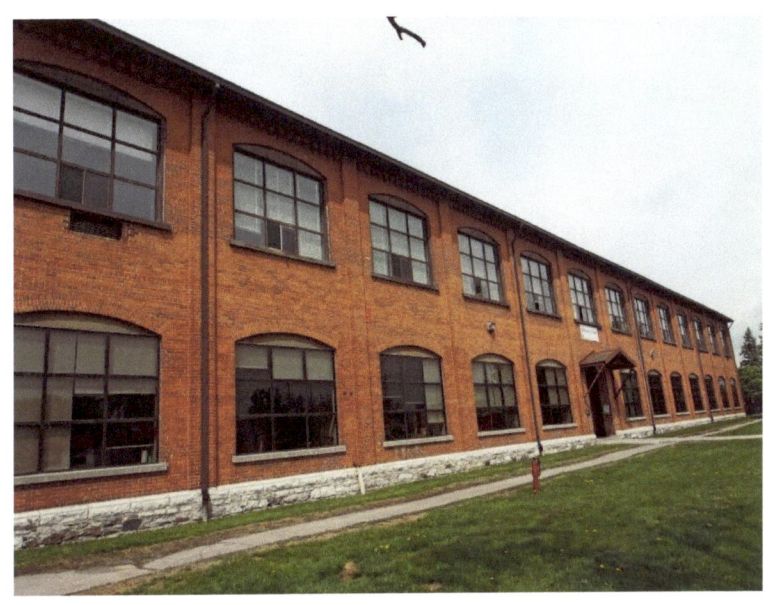

General Electric

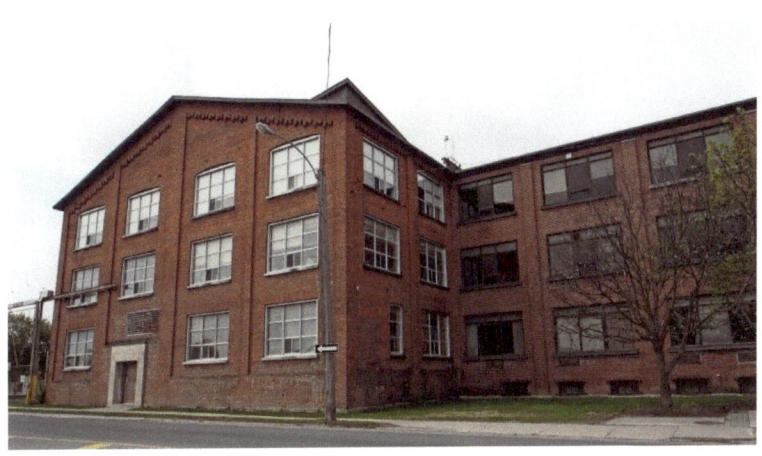

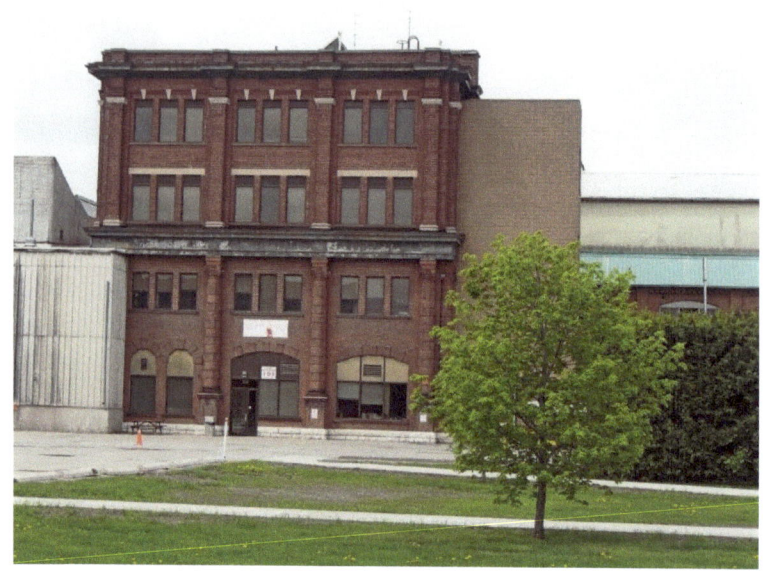

General Electric

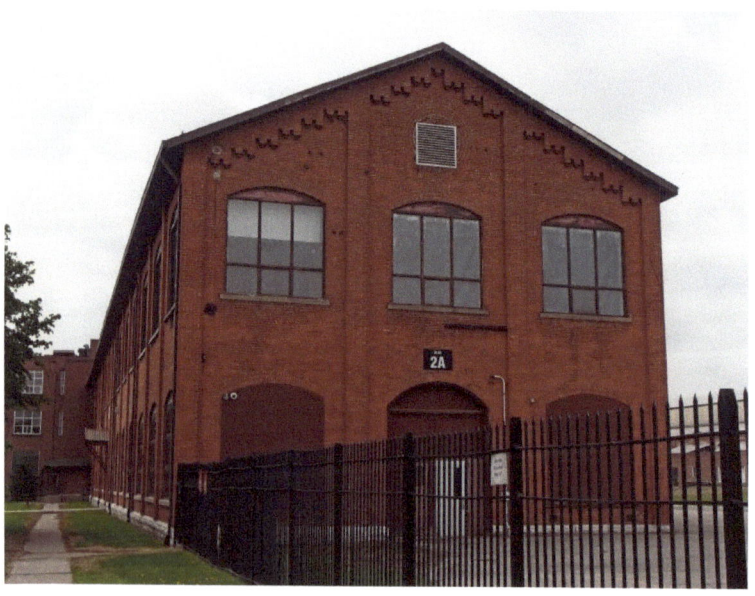

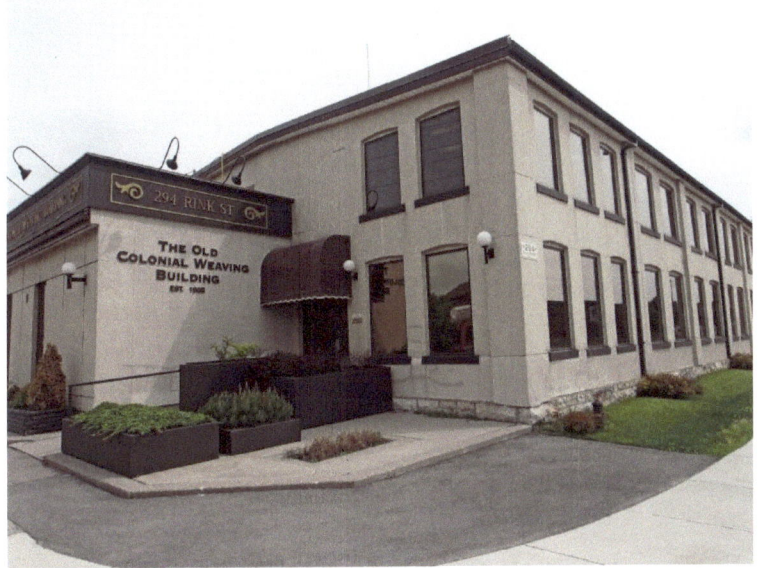

294 Rink Street – The Old Colonial Weaving Building
Established 1905

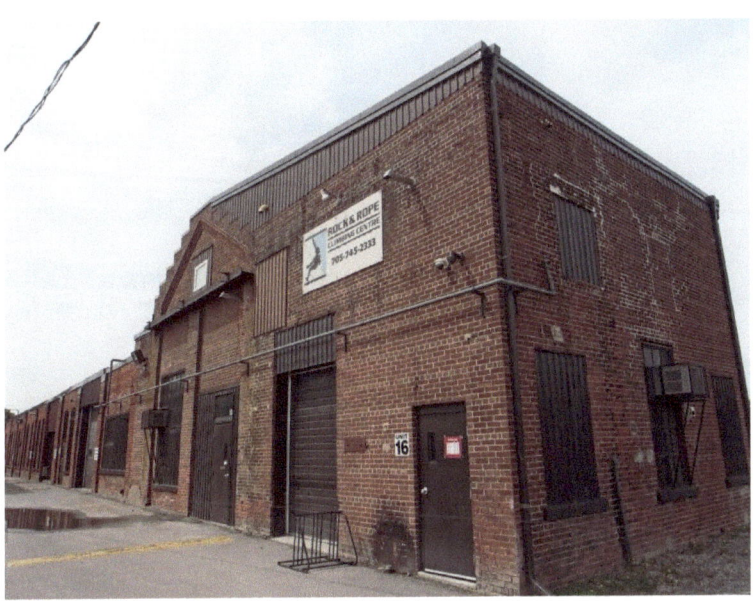

Rink Street

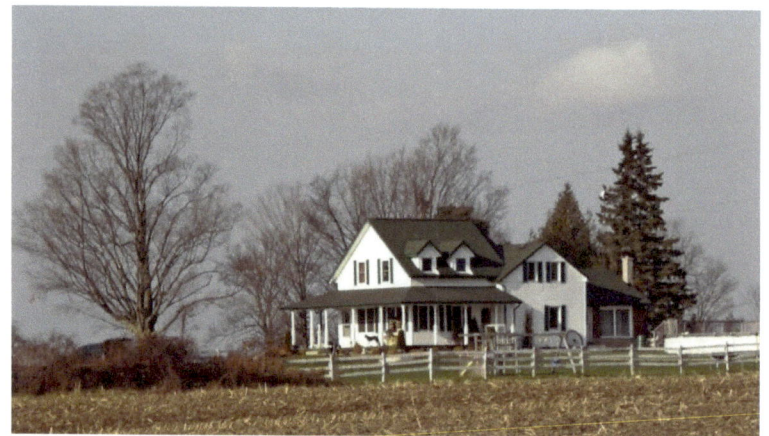

Gothic

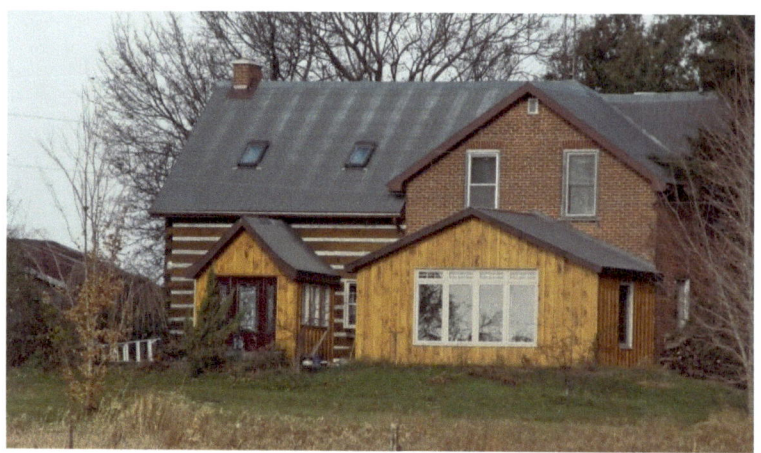

Log cabin

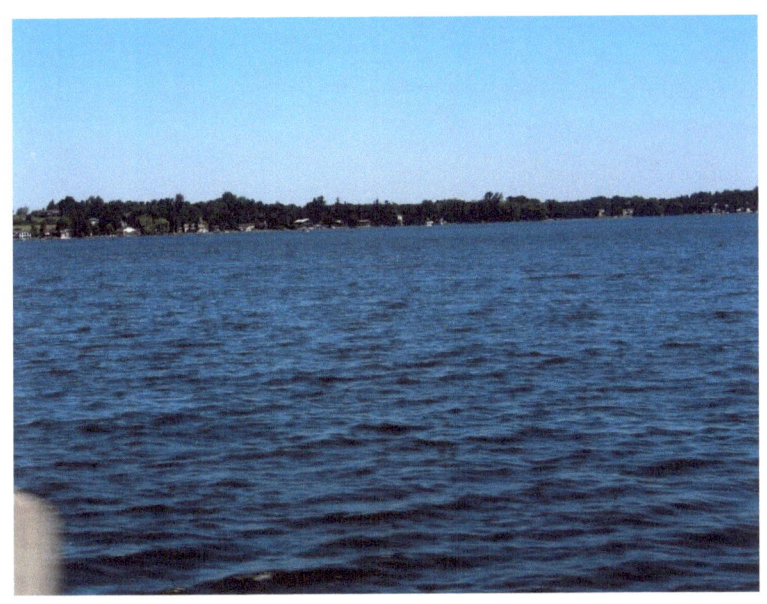

Chemong Lake from causeway at Bridgenorth

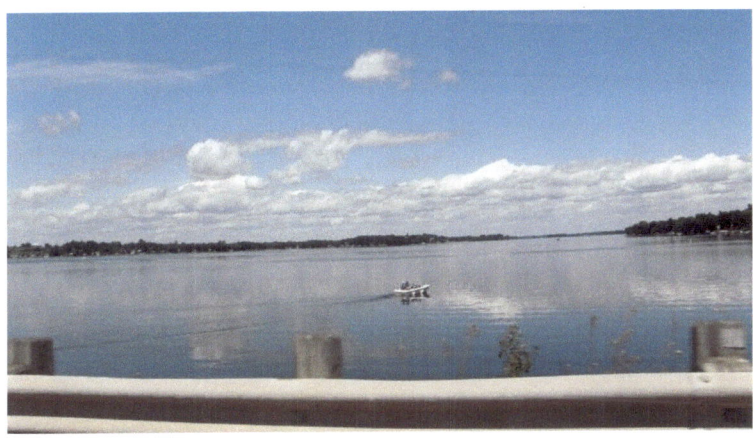

Bridgenorth

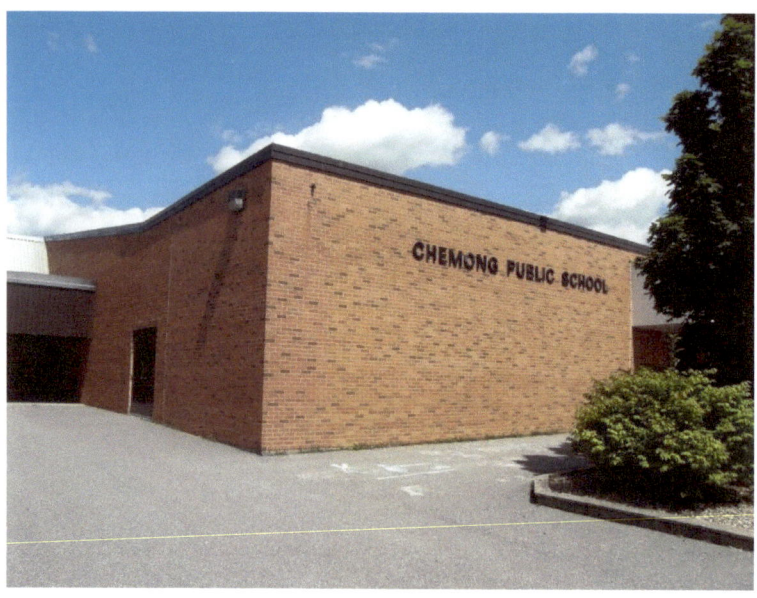

Chemong Public School with mural of original school

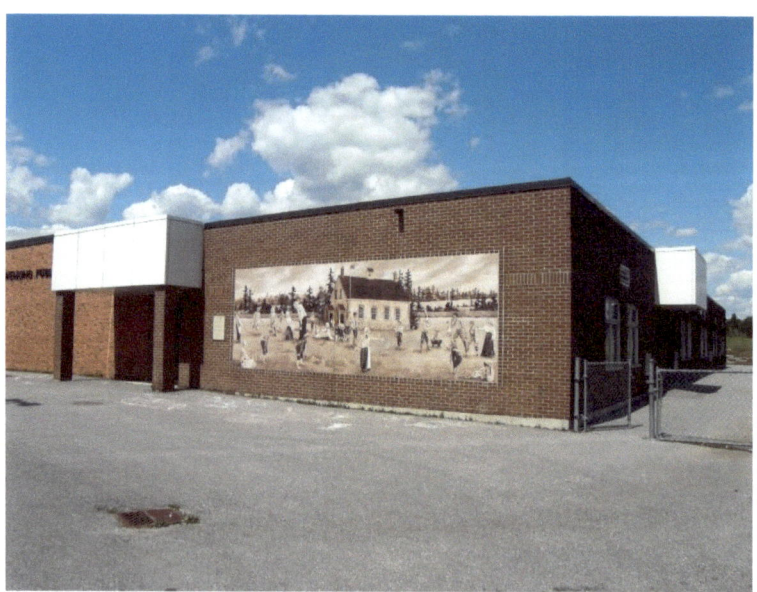

The red brick school house was a focal point in many nineteenth century Ontario communities. Smith Township was divided into seven school districts in 1873, with the Bridgenorth section named #5. The school property on Colborne Street was purchased for $125 and the school building with two water closets and a wood shed cost $1,025. S.S. No. 5 was completed in August 1876. The community held a picnic to celebrate the opening.

For many years, children living in school section #5 attended the one room school house for all grades, receiving an education typical of the time. The mid-twentieth century saw expansion of the original school, and the opening of the Gore Street site, and resulted in S.S. No. 5 being renamed Chemong Public School. The original school house was in use continually as a classroom until June 2002 – 126 years of learning.

Richard Hayman, Director of the Art School of Peterborough, was commissioned by Chemong School Council to paint the mural during the summer of 2002 to honour the little red school house that so many children have attended. Assisted by artist Donna Bolam, Richard has created an imaginative portrayal of recess circa 1876.

Students at Chemong modeled for the mural in 2002. They are all descendants of original Bridgenorth area families. Old family names represented include Bell, Jopling, Kelly, Mann, McIlmoyle, McManus, McWilliams, Nichols, Northey, Robinson, and Wood.

The mural was unveiled at the opening of the primary addition of Chemong Public School on October 2, 2002. The community spirit of the one room school will live on in Bridgenorth.

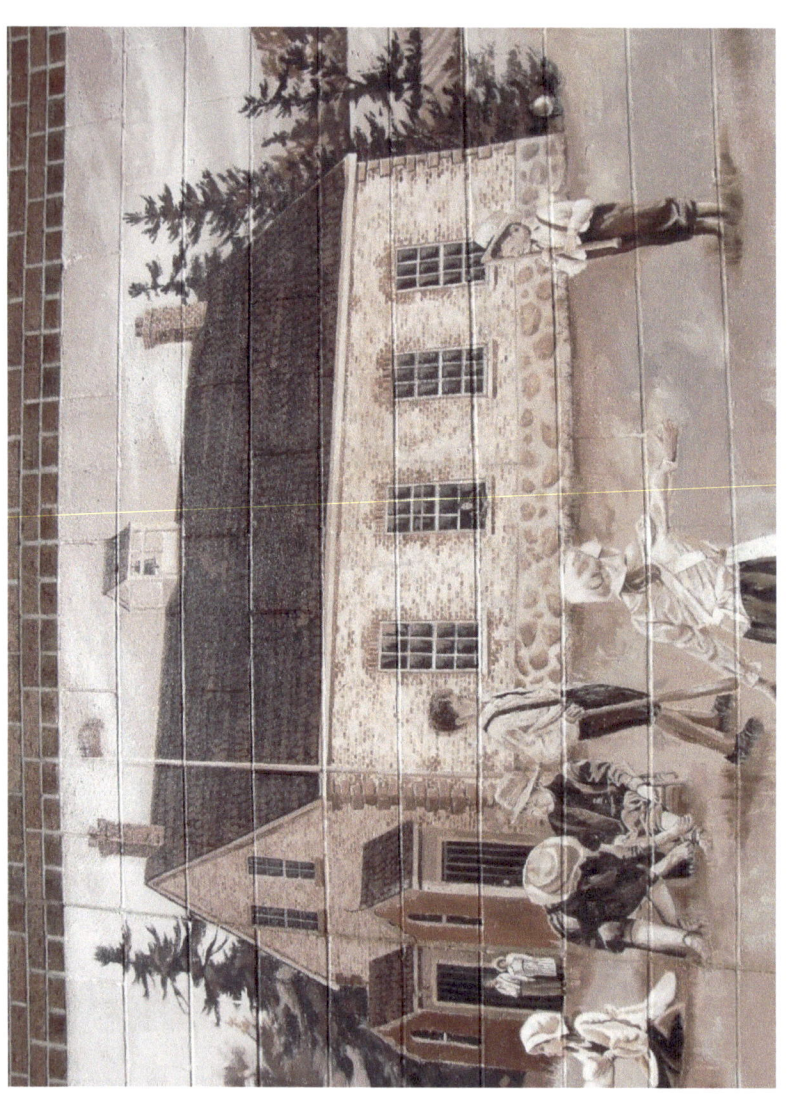

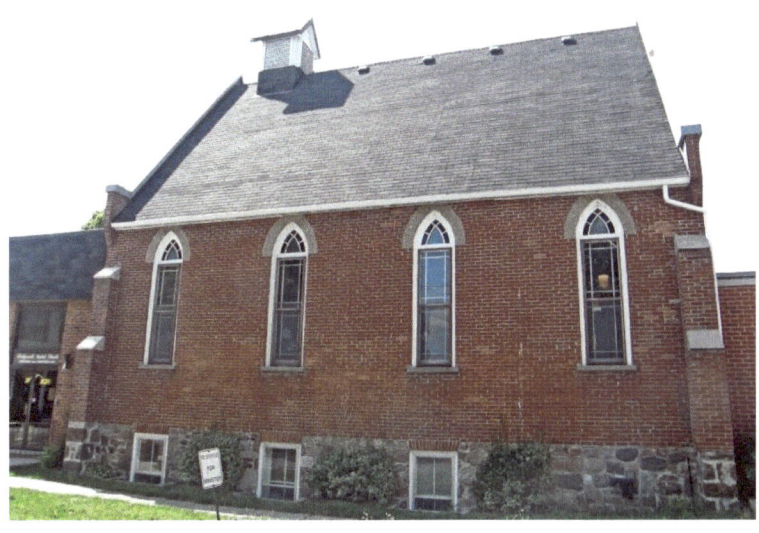

Bridgenorth United Church, founded 1842, erected 1889
Lancet windows, cobblestone basement wall

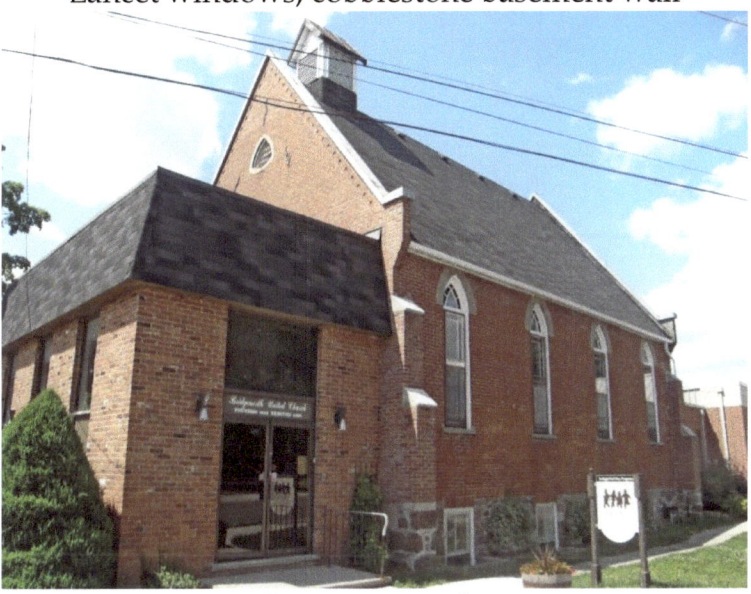

Buttress, cupola

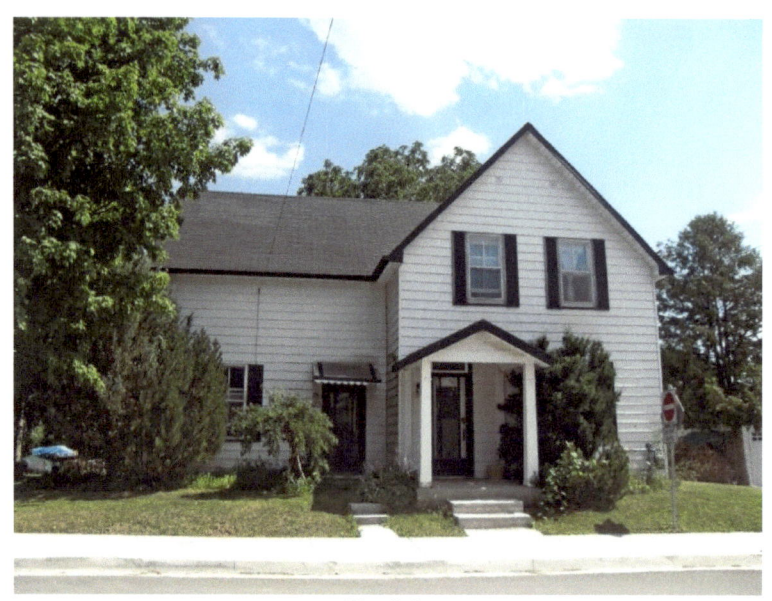

Gothic

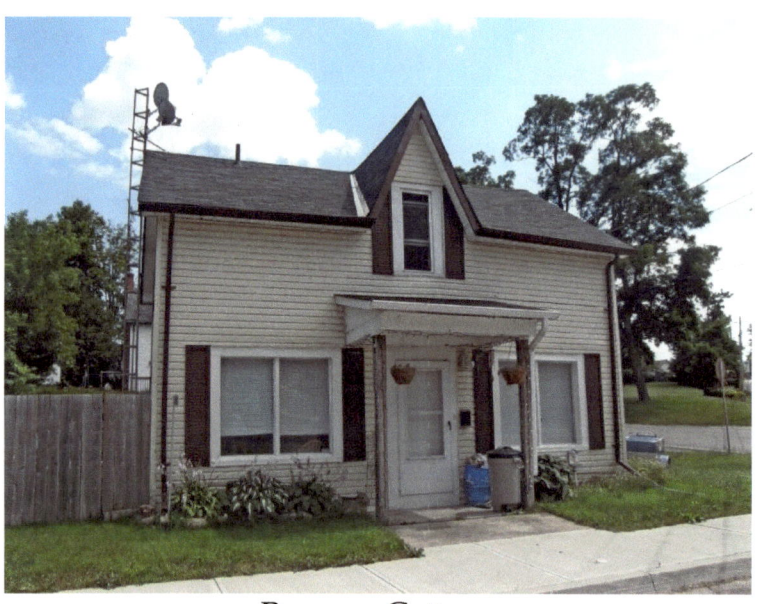

Regency Cottage

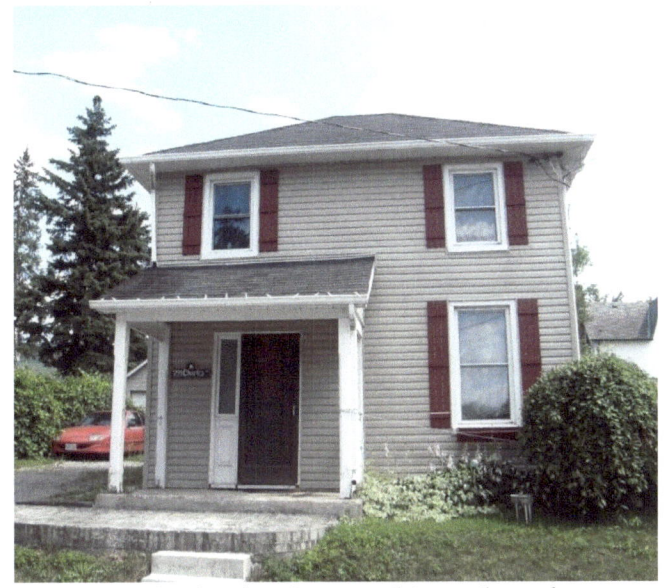

799 Charles Street – hipped roof

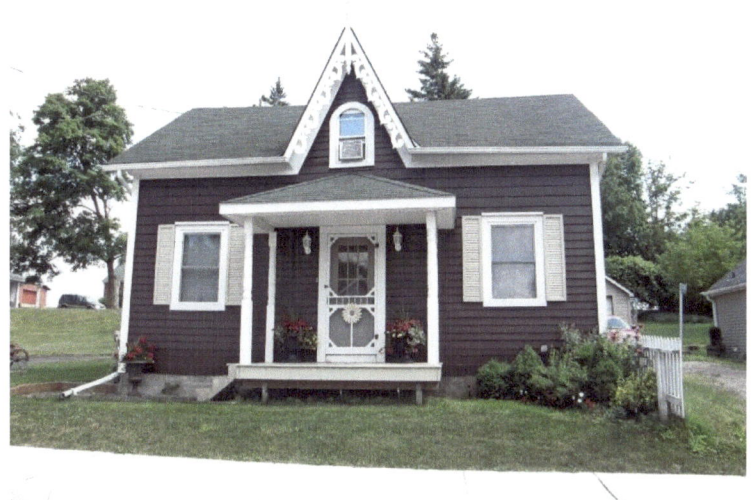

Regency Cottage

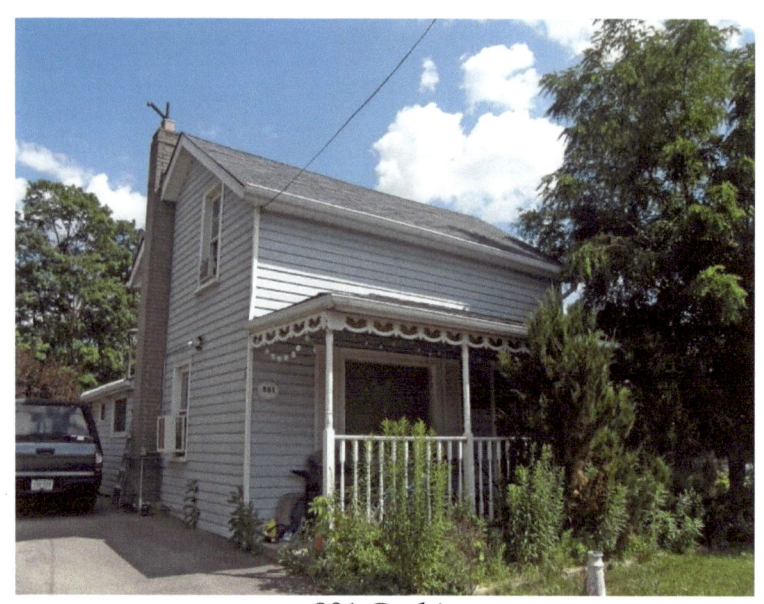

801 Gothic

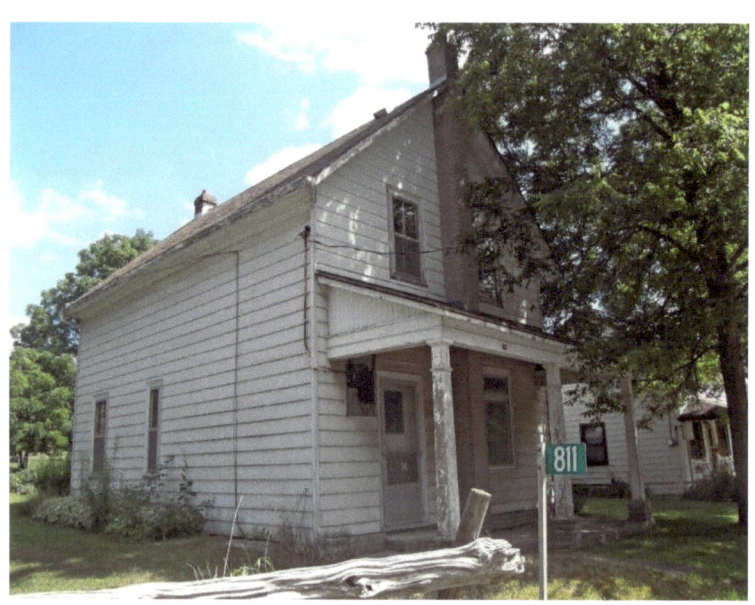

#811 - Gothic

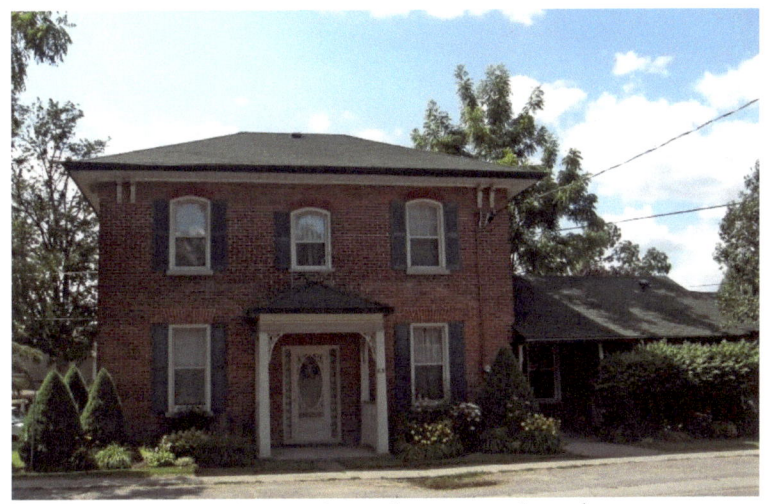

#808 – hipped roof, cornice brackets

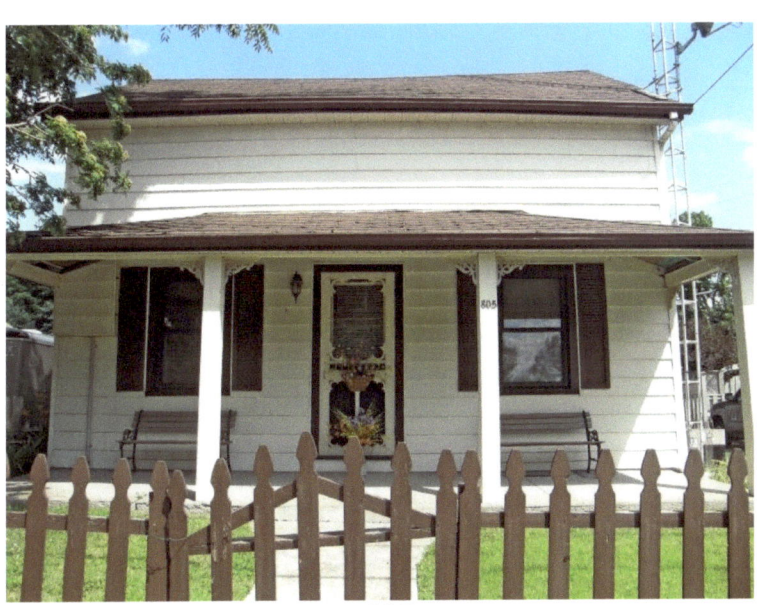

#805

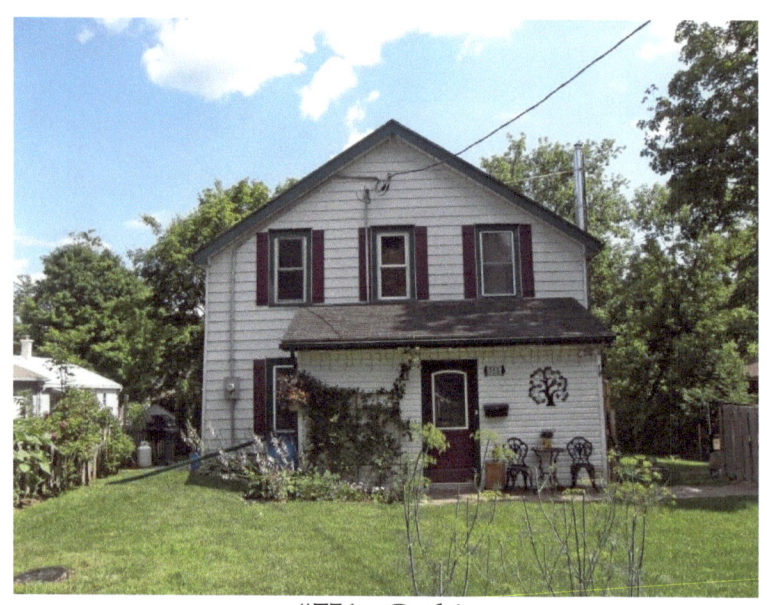

#751 - Gothic

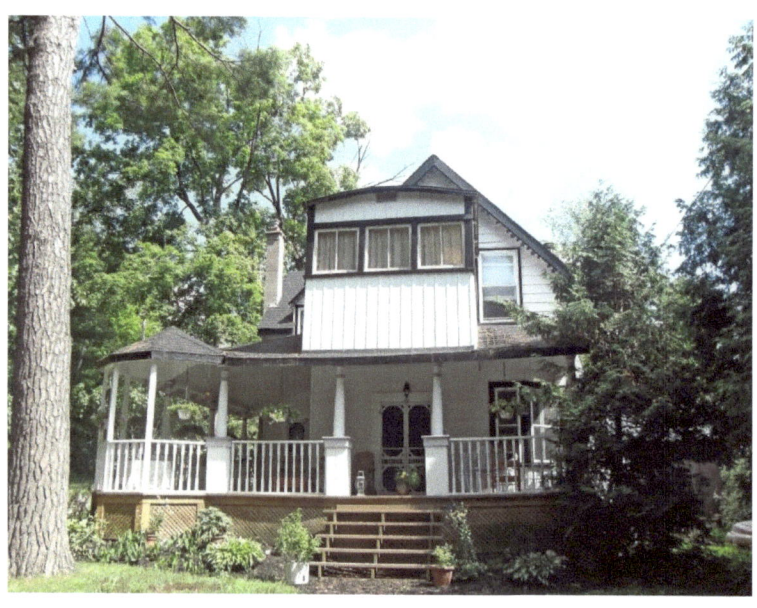

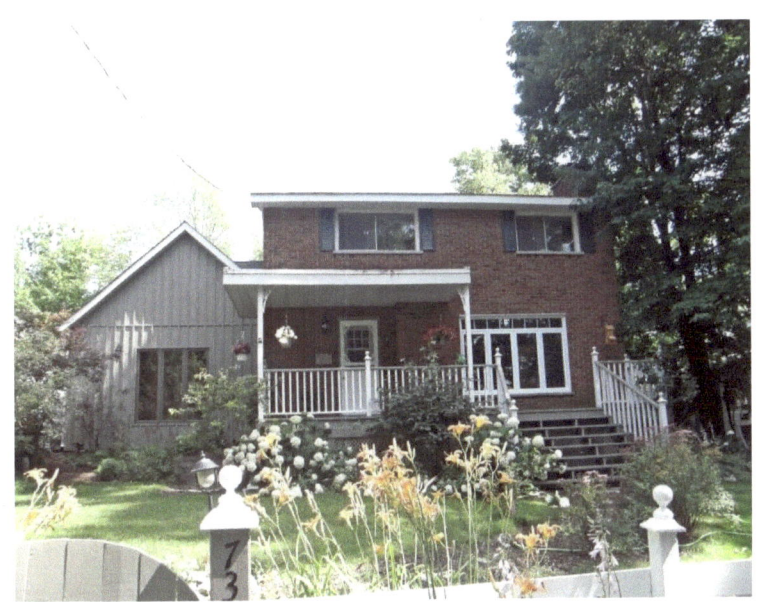

#73_

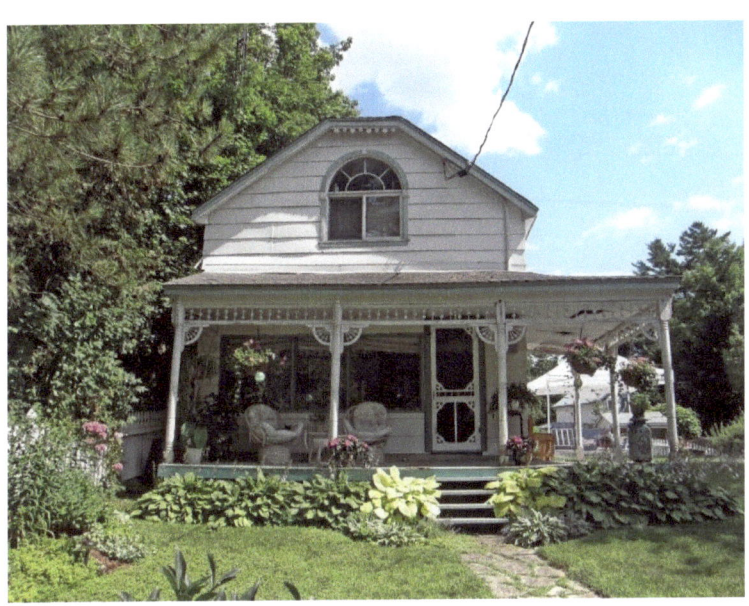

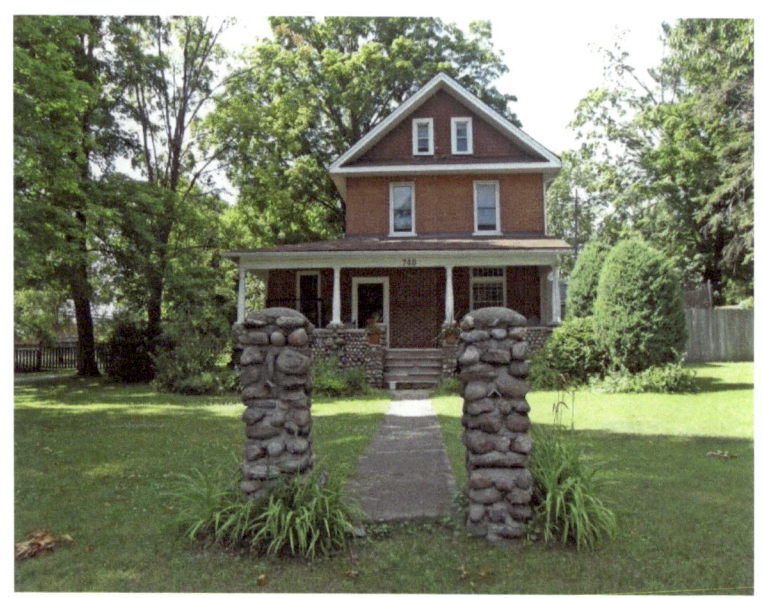

#748

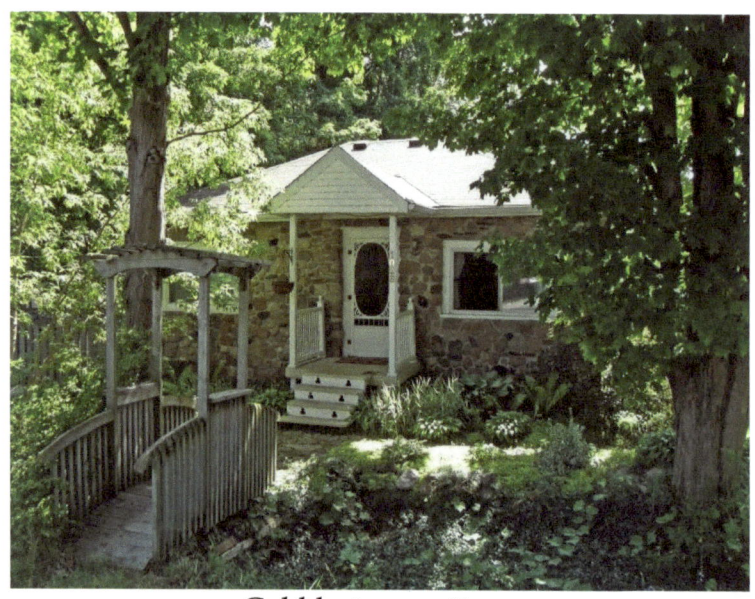

Cobblestone cottage

Emerald Isle

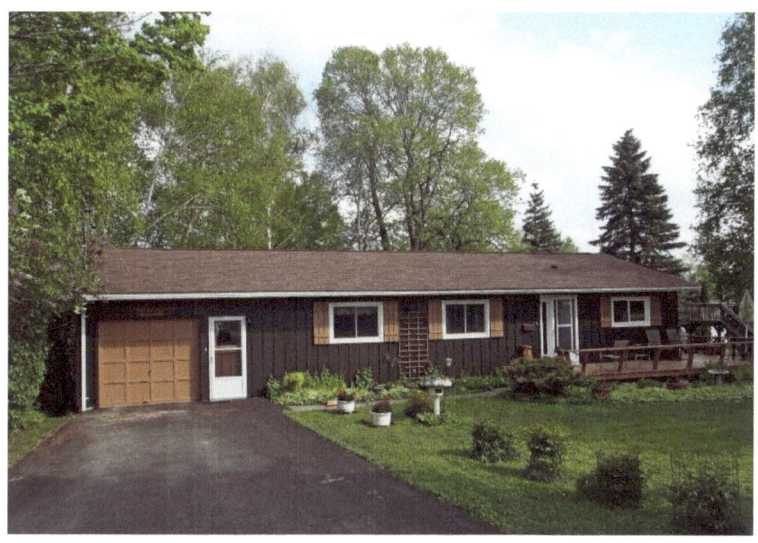

Home of Art and Iris Frankum, Cow Island

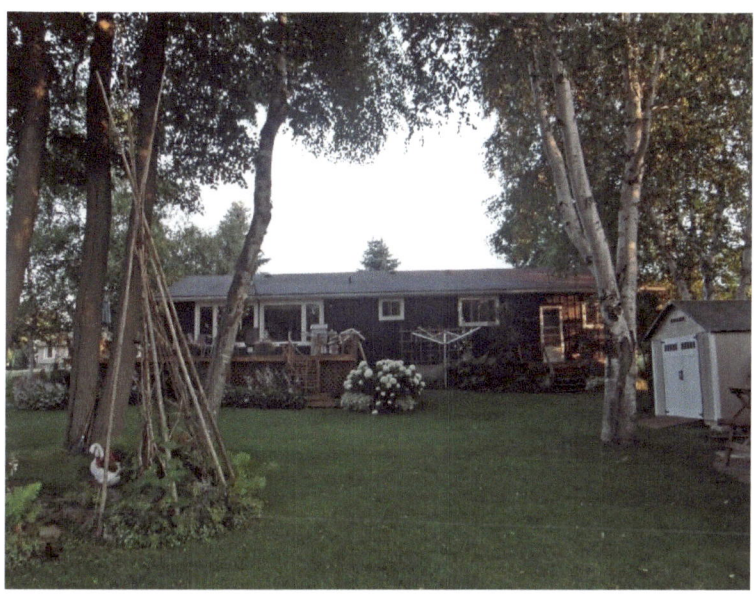

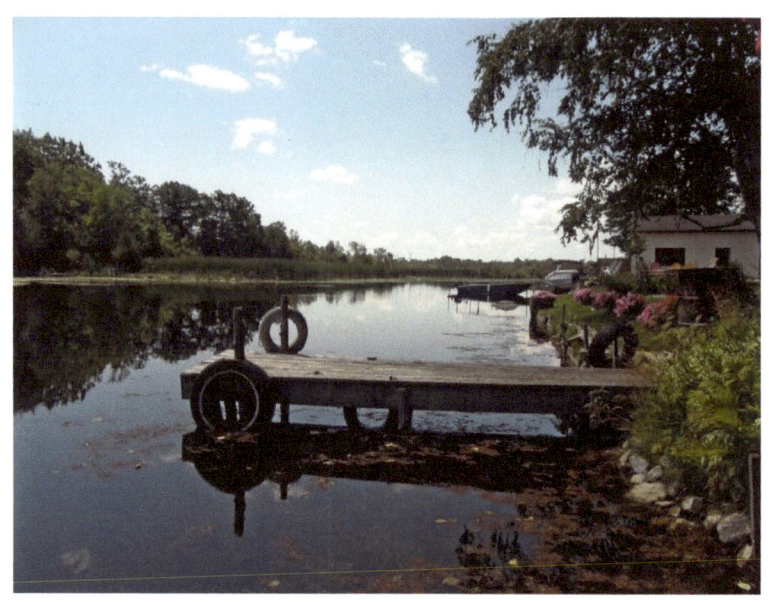

Reflections – Cow Island

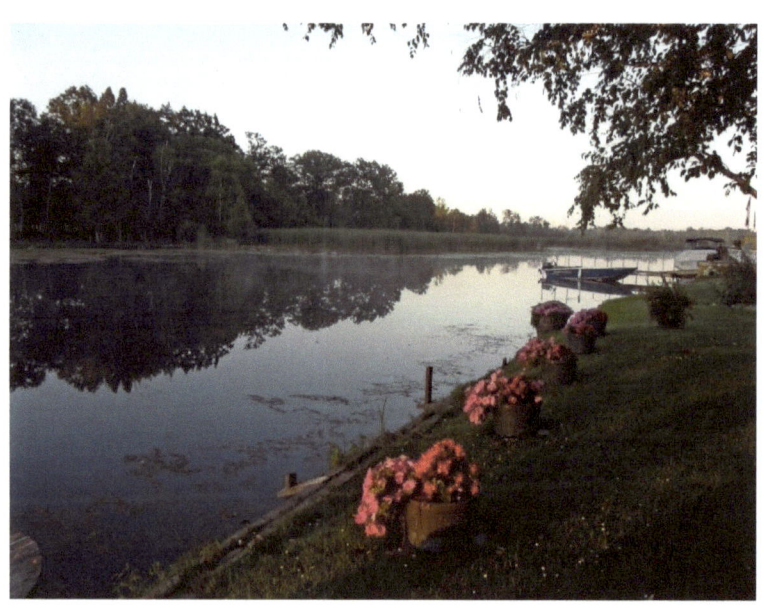

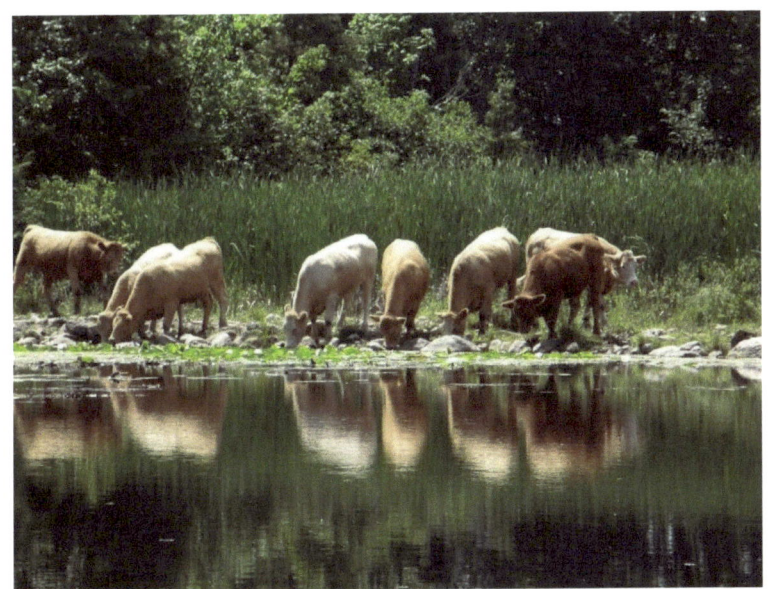

Cow Island

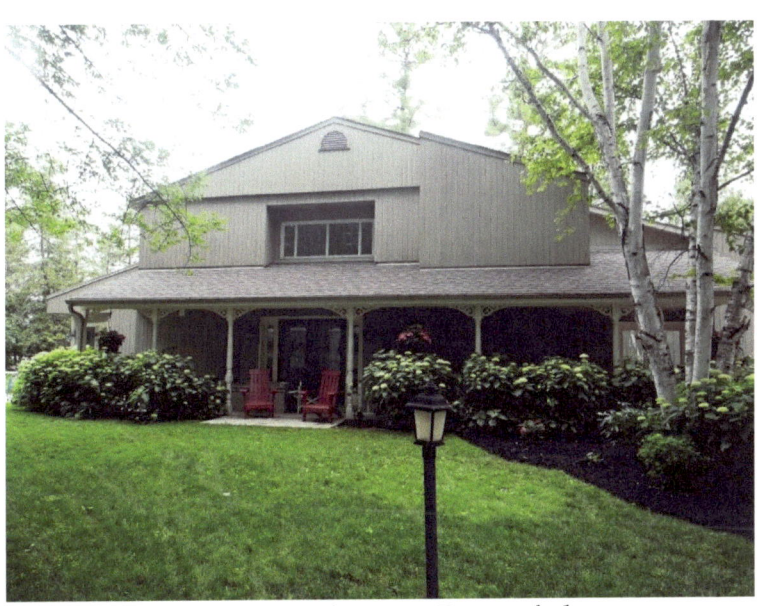

View of Pat and Harry Burton's house

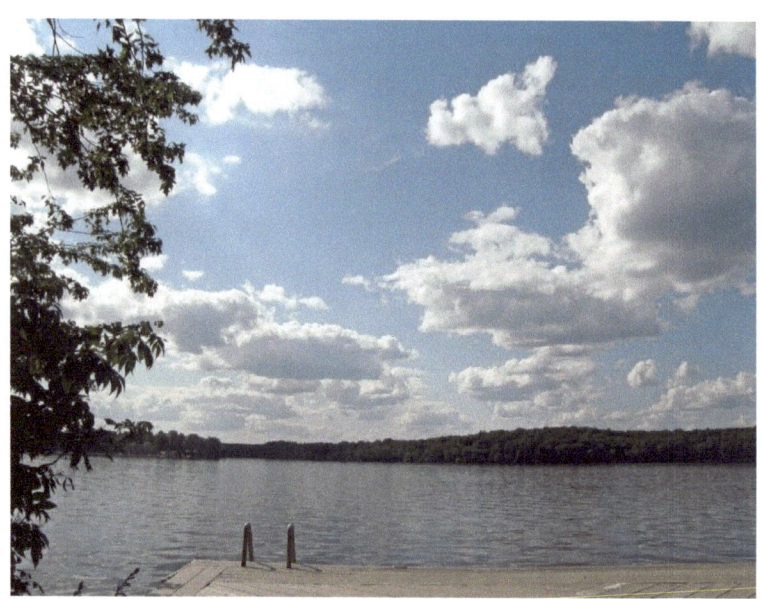

Buckhorn Lake from Burtons' dock

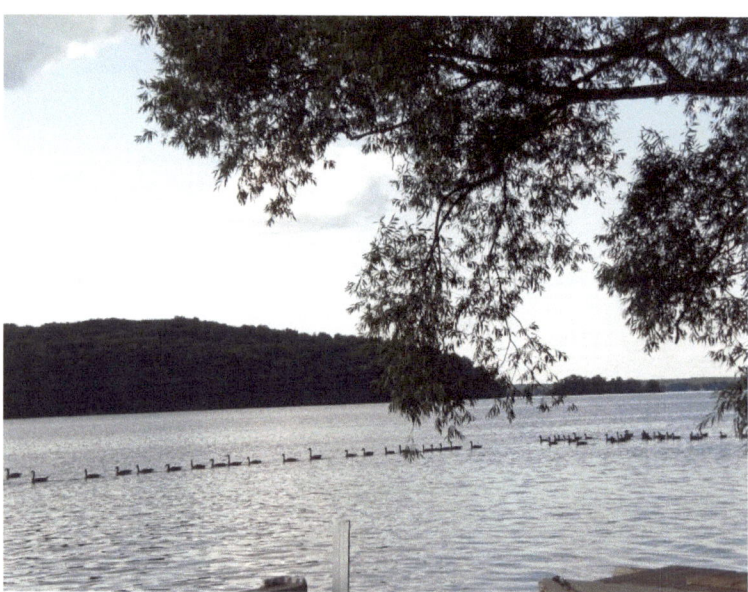

Geese on Buckhorn Lake

Ennismore

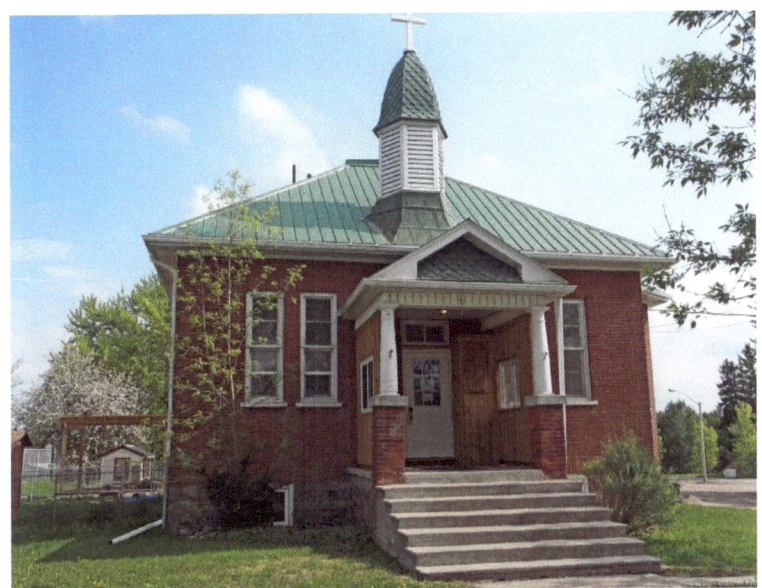

Pediment, turret

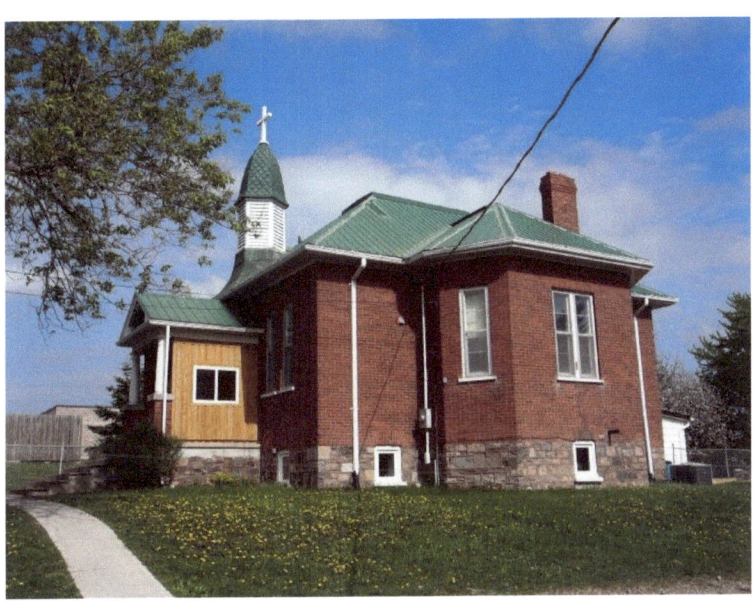

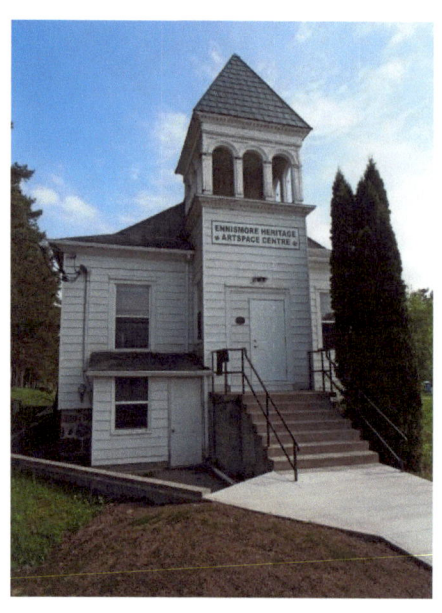

St. Martin's Parish Hall 1904

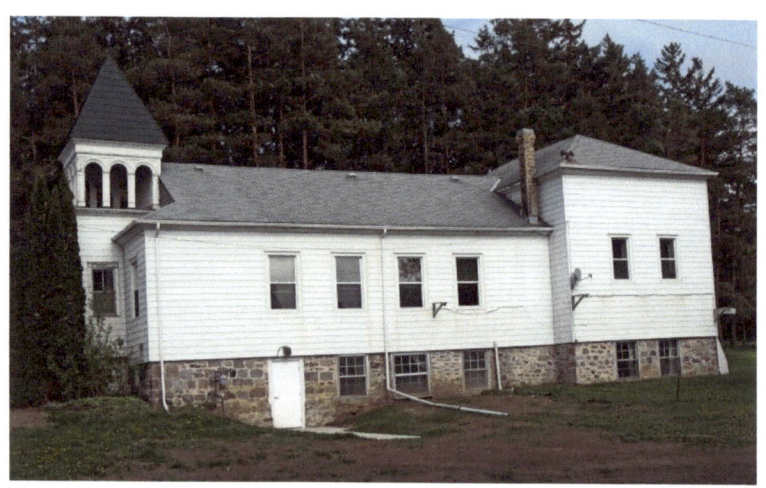

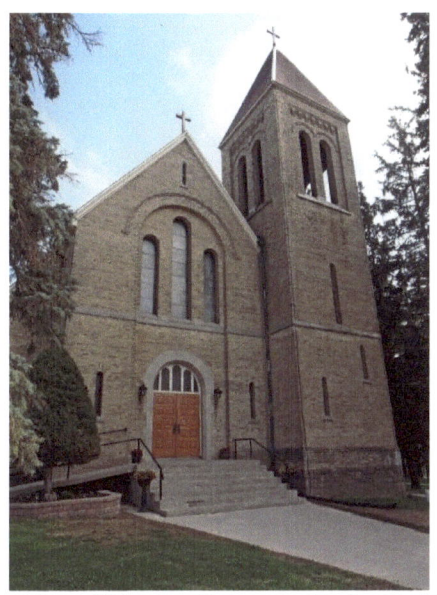

St. Martin of Tours Roman Catholic Parish
Gothic, buttresses, banding, lancet windows

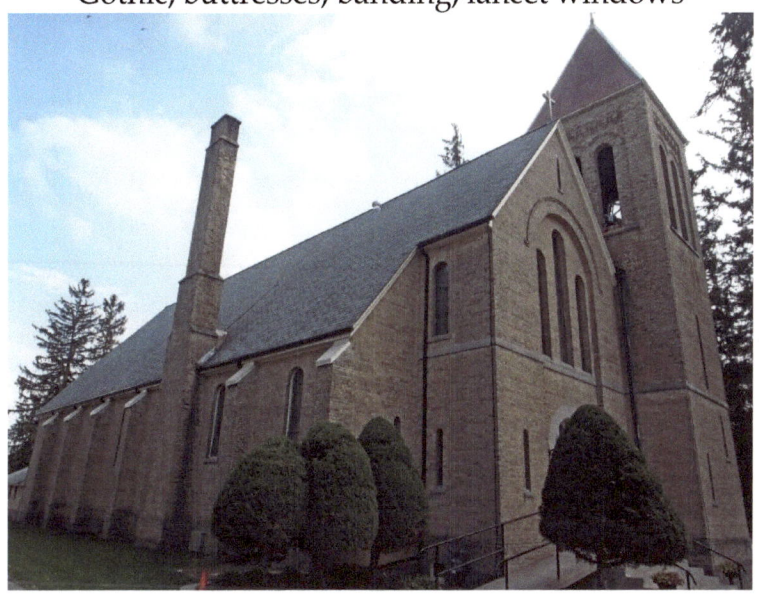

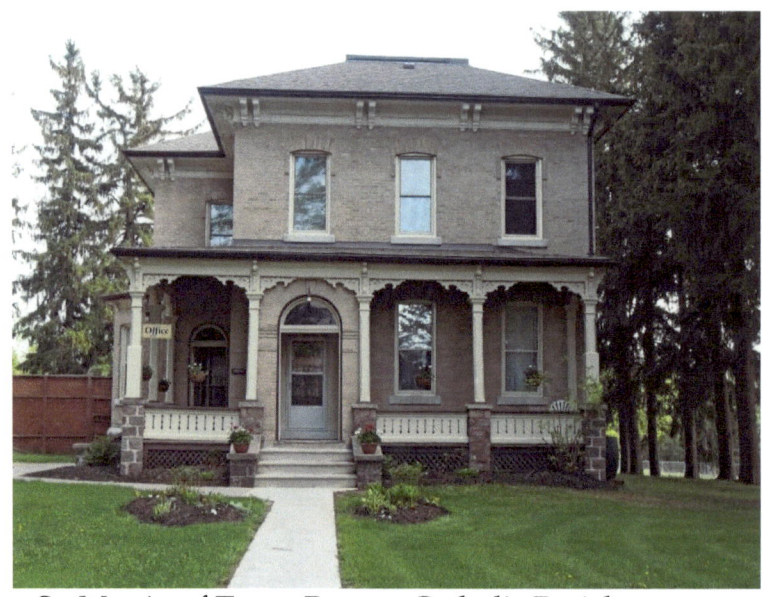

St. Martin of Tours Roman Catholic Parish - manse
Italianate, hipped roof, cornice brackets

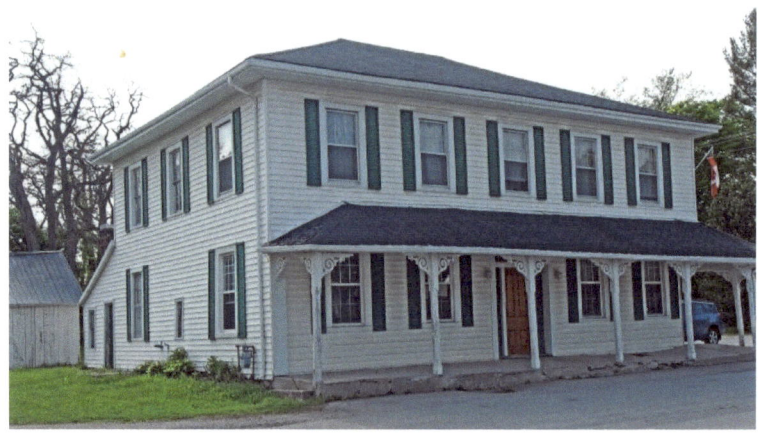

Georgian

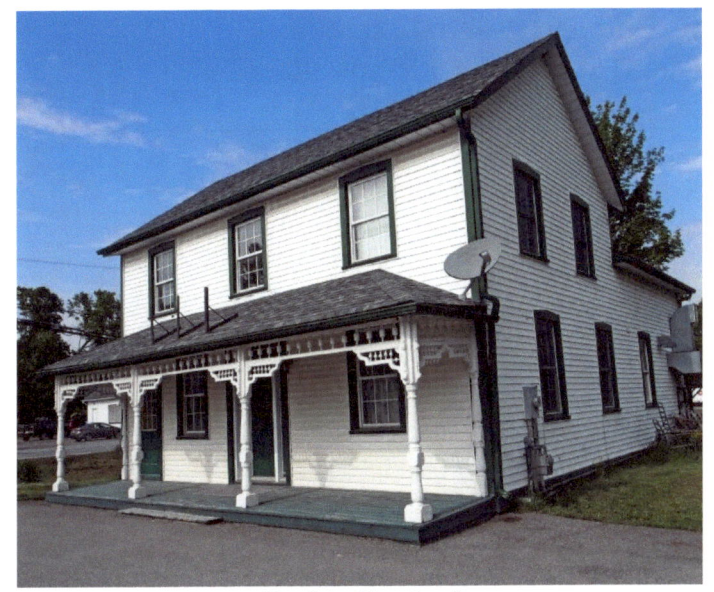

Gothic Revival

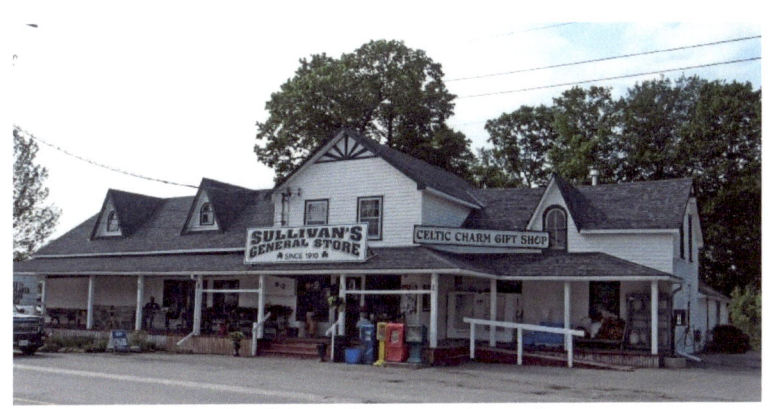

Gothic – dormers in attic

Banding: Different materials, colours or textures used in horizontal bands along a wall. Example: see Page 55	
Brackets: a decorative or weight-bearing structural element which forms a right angle with one side against a wall and the other under a projecting surface such as an eave or roof. Example: Ennismore, see Page 56	
Buttress: a masonry structure built against or projecting from a wall which serves to support or reinforce the wall. In Canadian architecture, they are sometimes used for decoration. Example: see Page 26	
Capital: The uppermost finish or decoration on a column. An Ionic column has a small base, a thin elegant shaft, and a capital composed of volutes which are carved whirls or twists that take the form of a scroll. Example: George Street City Hall	
Cobblestone architecture: Refers to the use of cobblestones embedded in mortar as a method for erecting walls on houses and commercial buildings. Example: Bridgenorth United Church, Pg. 41	
Cupola: A domed or curved roof rising from a building as a decorative element. Example: see Page 41	

Dormer: (French for "sleep") a gable end window that pierces through the plane of a sloping roof surface to create usable space in the top floor or attic of a building by adding headroom. Example: see Page 57	
Fretwork: interlaced decorative design resembling a bracket Example: 351 Park Street	
Gable: the triangular portion of a wall between the edges of a sloping roof. Example: 88 London Street	
Hipped Roof: a roof where all sides slope downwards to the walls with no gables.	
Iron Cresting: A decorative ornament along the top of a roof. Iron cresting was popular in the Baroque era and also in Italianate, Victorian, Second Empire and Queen Anne styles of architecture. Example: 351 Park Street	
Keystones and Voussoirs: a voussoir is a wedge-shaped element used in building an arch. A keystone is the central stone that locks all the stones into position, allowing the arch to bear weight. A keystone is often enlarged and embellished. Example: 548 George Street	
Lancet Window: a tall, narrow window with a pointed arch at its top. Example: Bridgenorth United Church, See Page 41	

Pediment: a triangular section above the horizontal structure (entablature), typically supported by columns. The inside of the triangle is called the tympanum. Example: George Street City Hall	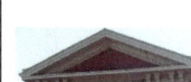
Turret: a small tower that projects from the wall of a building. Example: Ennismore, see Page 53	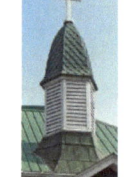
Verge board and Finial: also called bargeboards – hang from the projecting end of a roof and are often elaborately carved and ornamented. **Finial:** ornament added to the top of a gable, pinnacle, canopy or spire – a Gothic element. Example of finial: 533 Harvey Street	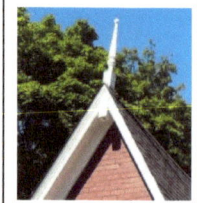

Building Styles

Edwardian, 1900-1930 – This style bridges the ornate and elaborate styles of the Victorian era and the simplified styles of the 20th century. Balanced facades, simple roof lines, dormer windows, large front porches, and smooth brick surfaces are its characteristics. Example: 404 Belmont Avenue	
Georgian, before 1860 – This style began with the British King Georges in the 18th century. These buildings have balanced facades around a central door, medium-pitched gable roofs, and small paned windows. Example: Ennismore, see Page 56	
Gothic Revival, 1830-1890 – These decorative buildings have sharply-pitched gables with highly detailed verge boards, pointed-arch window openings, and dichromatic brickwork. It is a common style in Ontario. Example: Harvey Street, see Page 18	
Italianate, 1850-1900 – It has wide-bracketed eaves, belvederes, wrap-around verandahs. Example: see Page 56	

A log cabin, built from logs, was usually one- or 1½-storeys constructed with round rather than hewn, or hand-worked, logs, and erected quickly for frontier shelter. Log cabins were built from logs laid horizontally and interlocked on the ends with notches. Careful notching minimized the size of the gap between the logs and reduced the amount of chinking with sticks and rocks or daubing with mud to fill the gap. Example: see Page 36	
Queen Anne, 1885-1900 – This style is distinguished by an irregular outline featuring a combination of an offset tower, broad gables, projecting two-storey bays, verandahs, multi-sloped roofs, and tall, decorative chimneys. A mixture of brick and wood is common. Windows often have one large single-paned bottom sash and small panes in the upper sash. Example: see Page 26	
Regency Cottage, 1830-1860 – This style originated in England in 1815 and spread to Ontario later in the 19th century as British officers retired to Canada. It is a modest one-storey house with a low-pitched hip roof and has a symmetrical front façade. Example: see Page 43	
Romanesque Revival, 1880-1910 – This style hearkens back to medieval architecture of the 11th and 12th centuries with a heavy appearance, blocky towers and rounded arches. Example: McDonnel Street, Peterborough Collegiate	

www.ingramcontent.com/pod-product-compliance
Lightning Source LLC
Chambersburg PA
CBHW040842180526
45159CB00001B/289